MW01259836

HEROES OF THE MIDDLE AGES

KING ARTHUR

HEROES OF THE MIDDLE AGES

(ALARIC TO JOAN OF ARC)

BY

EVA MARCH TAPPAN

YESTERDAY'S CLASSICS

CHAPEL HILL, NORTH CAROLINA

This edition, first published in 2006 by Yesterday's Classics, is an unabridged republication of the work originally published by George G. Harrap & Co. in 1911. For a complete listing of the books published by Yesterday's Classics, please visit www.yesterdaysclassics.com. Yesterday's Classics is the publishing arm of the Baldwin Project which presents the complete text of dozens of classic books for children at www.mainlesson.com under the editorship of Lisa M. Ripperton and T. A. Roth.

ISBN-10: 1-59915-169-3

ISBN-13: 978-1-59915-169-4

Yesterday's Classics
PO Box 3418
Chapel Hill, NC 27515

PREFACE

I HAVE sometimes wondered if every one realizes how startlingly independent and isolated a historical fact is to the young reader. It has happened before his remembrance, and that alone is enough to put it into another world. It is outside of his own experience. It has appeared to him by no familiar road, but from unknown regions of space.

The object of this book is to bring together stories of the most important movements in the history of Europe during the Middle Ages, and to make familiar the names of the most important figures in those scenes. I have endeavoured to weave a tapestry in which, with due colour, may be traced the history of the rise and fall of the various nationalities and the circumstances and mode of life of each—in short, to give the young reader an approximation to the background for the study of his country's history which a wide reading gives to a man.

EVA MARCH TAPPAN

CONTENTS

THE FIRST PERIOD
THE BARBARIAN INVASION

THE SECOND PERIOD
THE FORMING OF THE GERMANIC NATIONS

THE THIRD PERIOD
THE TEUTONIC INVASIONS

THE FOURTH PERIOD
THE RISE OF NATIONALITIES

THE FIFTH PERIOD
THE CRUSADES

THE SIXTH PERIOD
THE TIME OF PROGRESS AND DISCOVERY

THE SEVENTH PERIOD
THE STRUGGLES OF THE NATIONS

CHAPTER I

ALARIC THE VISIGOTH

But thou, imperial City! thou hast stood
In greatness once, in sackcloth now and tears,
A mighty name, for evil or for good,
Even in the loneness of thy widowed years:
Thou that hast gazed, as the world hurried by,
Upon its headlong course with sad prophetic eye.

MATTHEW ARNOLD

IF an Italian country boy had been taken to visit Rome fifteen hundred years ago, he would have found much to see. There were temples and theatres and baths. There were aqueducts, sometimes with arches one hundred feet high, stretching far out into the country to bring pure water to the city. There was an open space known as the Forum, where the people came together for public meetings, and in this space were beautiful pillars and arches and statues of famous Romans. Around the Forum were palaces and temples and the Senate House; and directly in front of the Senate House was a platform on which speakers stood when they wished to address the people. The platform was called the rostrum, which is a Latin word, meaning the beak of a

1

warship, because it was adorned with the beaks of ships which the Romans had captured. Another open space was the great race-course, the Circus Maximus, in which 250,000 people could sit and watch leaping, wrestling, boxing, foot-races, and especially the famous four-horse chariot races. There was the Coliseum, too, where gladiators, generally captives or slaves, fought with one another or with wild beasts.

The Roman streets were narrow, and they seemed still narrower because many houses were built with their upper stories projecting over the lower; but in those narrow streets there was always something of interest. Sometimes it was a wedding procession with torches and songs and the music of the flute. Sometimes it was a funeral train with not only the friends of the dead man, but also trumpeters and pipers. In the long line walked hired actors wearing waxen masks made to imitate the faces of the dead person's ancestors. Early in the morning, one could see crowds of clients, each one hastening to the home of his patron, some wealthy man who was expected to give him either food or money.

Rome was built upon seven hills, and most of these men of wealth lived either on the Palatine or the Esquiline Hill. After a patron had received his clients, he ate a light meal and then attended to his business, if he had any. About noon he ate another meal and had a nap. When he awoke, he played ball or took some other exercise. Then came his bath; and this was quite a lengthy affair, for there was not only hot and cold bathing, but there was rubbing and scraping and anointing. At the public baths were hot rooms and cold rooms and rooms where friends might sit and talk together, or lie on couches and rest. Dinner, the principal meal of the day, came at two or three o'clock. Oysters were often served first, together with radishes, lettuce, sorrel, and pickled cabbage. These were to increase the keenness of the appetite. Then came fish, flesh, and fowl, course after course. Next came cakes and fruits, and last, wine followed, mixed with water and spices. The formal banquets were much more elaborate than this, for a good host must load his table with as many kinds of expensive food as possible; and a guest who wished to show his appreciation must eat as much as he could. The whole business of a feast was eating, and there was seldom any witty conversation. No one sung any songs or told any merry stories.

Such was the life of the wealthy Romans. Moreover, they kept hosts of slaves to save themselves from every exertion. Their ancestors had been brave, patriotic folk who loved their country and thought it was an honour to fight for it; but these idle, luxurious people were not willing to give up their comfort and leisure and to enter the army. Hired soldiers could defend their fatherland, they thought.

The time had come when Rome needed to be defended. In the early days, it had been only a tiny settlement, but it had grown in power till the Romans ruled all Europe south of the Rhine and the Danube, also Asia Minor, Northern Africa, and Britain. Nearly all the people of Europe are thought to have come from Central Asia. One tribe after another moved to the westward from their early home into Europe, and when the hunting and fishing became poor in their new settlements, they went on still farther west. The Celts came first, pushing their way through Central Europe, and finally into France, Spain, and the British Isles. Later, the Latins and Greeks took possession of Southern Europe. Meanwhile the Celts had to move faster than they wished into France, Spain, and Britain, because another race, the Teutons, had followed close behind them, and taken possession of Central Europe. These Teutons, who lived a wild, restless, half-savage life, roamed back and forth between the Danube and the shores of the Baltic Sea. They consisted of many different tribes, but the Romans called them all Germans. For many years the Germans had tried to cross the Danube and the Rhine, and break into the Roman Empire, but the Roman armies had driven them back, and had destroyed their rude villages again and again. Sometimes, however, the Germans were so stubborn in their efforts to get into the empire that the Roman emperors found it convenient to admit certain tribes as allies.

As time went on, a tribe of Teutons called Goths became the most troublesome of all to the Romans. Part of them lived on the shores of the Black Sea, and were called Ostrogoths, or Eastern Goths; while those who lived near the shores of the Danube were called Visigoths, or Western Goths. Toward the end of the fourth century, the Visigoths found themselves between two fires, for another people, the Huns, were driving them into the Roman Empire, and the Romans were driving them back. The Visigoths could not fight both nations, and in despair they sent ambassadors to the Romans. "Let us live on your side of the river," they pleaded. "Give us food, and we will defend the frontier for you." The bargain was made, but it was broken by both parties. It had been agreed that the Goths should give up their arms, but they bribed the Roman officers and kept them. The Romans had promised to furnish food, but they did not keep their word. Hungry warriors with weapons in their hands make fierce enemies. The Goths revolted, and the Roman Emperor was slain.

ALARIC AT ATHENS

As the years passed, the Goths grew stronger and the Romans weaker. By and by, a man named Alaric became leader of the Visigoths. He and his followers had fought under Roman commanders. He had been in Italy twice, and he began to wonder whether it would not be possible for him and his brave warriors to fight their way into the heart of the Roman Empire. One night, he dreamed that he was driving a golden chariot through the streets of Rome and that the Roman citizens were thronging about him and shouting, "Hail, O Emperor, hail!" Another time when he was passing by a sacred grove, he heard, or thought he heard, a voice cry, "You will make your way to the city." "The city" meant Rome, of course; and now Alaric called his chief men together and laid his plans before them. First, they would go to Greece, he said. The warlike Goths shouted for joy, for in the cities of Greece were treasures of gold and silver, and these would fall into the hands of the victors. They went on boldly, and before long Alaric and his followers were feasting in Athens, while great masses of treasure were waiting to be distributed among the soldiers. The Greeks had forgotten how brave their ancestors had been, and Alaric had no trouble in sweeping over the country. At last, however, the general Stilicho was sent with troops from Rome; and now Alaric would have been captured or slain if he had not succeeded in slipping away. Before this, the Roman Empire had been divided into two parts, the western and the eastern. The capital of the western part was Rome; that of the eastern was Constantinople.

6

The young man of eighteen who was emperor in the eastern part of the empire became jealous of Stilicho. "If he wins more victories, he will surely try to make himself emperor," thought the foolish boy; and he concluded that it would be an exceedingly wise move to make Alaric governor of Eastern Illyricum. This was like setting a hungry cat to watch a particularly tempting little mouse; for Illyricum stretched along the Adriatic Sea, and just across the narrow water lay Italy. Of course, after a few years, Alaric set out for Italy. The boy emperor in the western part of the empire ran away as fast as he could go. He would have been captured had not Stilicho appeared. Then Alaric and his warriors held a council. "Shall we withdraw and make sure of the treasure that we have taken, or shall we push on to Rome?" questioned the warriors. "I will find in Italy either a kingdom or a grave," declared the chief; but Stilicho was upon them, and they were obliged to retreat. Then the boy emperor returned to Rome to celebrate the victory and declare that he had never thought of such a thing as being afraid. Nevertheless, he hurried away to a safe fortress again, and left Rome to take care of itself.

Alaric waited for six years, but meanwhile he watched everything that went on in Italy. The boy emperor had become a man of twenty-five, but he was as foolish as ever; and now, like the Emperor in the East, he concluded that Stilicho meant to become ruler of the empire, and he murdered the only man who could have protected it.

7

A BARBARIAN INVASION

This was Alaric's opportunity, and he marched straight up to the walls of Rome, shut off food from the city, and commanded it to surrender. The luxurious Romans were indignant that a mere barbarian should think of conquering their city. Even after they were weakened by famine and pestilence, they told Alaric that if he would give them generous terms of surrender, they might yield; "but if not," they said, "sound your trumpets and make ready to meet a countless multitude." Alaric laughed and retorted, "The thicker the hay, the easier it is mowed." He would leave Rome, he declared, if they would bring him all the gold and silver of the city. Finally, however, he agreed to accept 5000 pounds of gold, 30,000 pounds of silver, 4000 robes of silk, 3000 pieces of scarlet cloth, and 3000 pounds of pepper.

Only two years later, Alaric came again, and the proud Romans were ready to do whatever he commanded. This time he put the prefect of the city upon the throne; but a little later he came a third time and encamped before the walls of Rome. The trumpets blew blast after blast, and the invaders poured into the city. Alaric bade his men spare both churches and people; but the Goths killed all who opposed them, or whom they suspected of concealing their wealth. Then they went away loaded with gold and silver and silk and jewels. They were in no haste to leave Italy with its wine and oil and cattle and corn; and, moreover, Alaric was not satisfied with sacking Rome; he meant to get possession of Sicily and then make an expedition to Africa. Suddenly all these plans came to an end, for he was taken ill and died. His followers turned aside a little river from its channel, wrapped the body of their dead leader in the richest of the Roman robes, and made his grave in the river bed. They heaped around it the most splendid of their treasures, and then turned back the waters of the stream to flow over it for ever. Finally, lest the grave should become known and be robbed or treated with dishonour, they put to death the multitude of captives whom they had forced to do this work.

CHAPTER II

ATTILA THE HUN

WHILE Alaric was winning his victories, the Huns had built on the banks of the Danube what they looked upon as their capital. The homes of the poorer folk were huts of mud or straw; but the king Attila, and his chief men lived in houses of wood with columns finely carved and polished. There was plenty of some kinds of luxury in this strange capital, for the tables of the chiefs were loaded with golden dishes; and swords, shoes, and even the trappings of the horses gleamed with gold and sparkled with jewels. King Attila, however, would have no such elegance. "I live as did my ancestors," he declared; and in his wooden palace he wore only the plainest of clothes. He ate nothing but flesh, and he was served from rough wooden bowls and plates. Nevertheless, he was proud of his wealth because it had been taken from enemies, and so was a proof of the bravery and daring of his people.

This king of a barbarous tribe meant to become the greatest of conquerors. Even in the early years of his reign he had hoped to do this. It is said that one of his shepherds noticed one day that the foot of an ox was wet with blood. He searched for the cause, and discovered a sharp point of steel sticking up from the ground. He began to dig around it, and soon saw that it was a sword. "That must go to the king," he said to himself, and he set out for the palace. King Attila examined the weapon closely and declared, "This is the sword of Tyr. I will wear it as long as I live, for no one who wears the sword of the war-god can ever know defeat."

When Attila had made his preparations, he set out with his followers to conquer the world. Before long, Constantinople was in his power. The Emperor in the East called himself the Invincible Augustus, but he could not meet Attila, and to save his city and his life he had to give the barbarians 6000 pounds of gold and a large tract of land on the Roman side of the Danube.

Wherever Attila went, he was successful. His ferocious warriors rode like the wind. They would dash down upon some village, kill the inhabitants, snatch up whatever there was of booty, and level the homes of the people so completely that it was said a horse could gallop over the ruins without danger of stumbling. In the far East, he was thought to be a magician. "The Huns have a wonder-stone," declared the folk of that region, "and whenever they choose they can raise storms of wind or rain." It is no wonder that men trembled at the sound of Attila's name and shuddered at the thought of the Scourge of God, as he called himself, when they heard any strange sound in the night. "Attila and his

Huns are the children of demons," they whispered; and those who had seen them were ready to believe that this was true. They were of a different family from the Goths and Celts and Romans. They were short and thick-set, with big heads and dark, swarthy complexions. Their eyes were small and bright, and so deep-set that they seemed to be far back in their skulls. Their turned-up noses were so short and broad that it was commonly said they had no noses, but only two holes in their faces.

Although Attila had made peace with the Emperor in the East, before long he found an excuse for invading his empire. With the sword of Tyr in his hand, he swept across what is now Germany and France, killing and burning wherever he went. When he came to Orleans, he expected that city to yield as the others had done; but the people had just made their fortifications stronger, and they had no idea of surrendering even to the terrible Huns. But before long, Attila had got possession of the suburbs, he had weakened the walls with his battering-rams, and the people of Orleans began to tremble with fear. Those who could not bear arms were at the altars praying, and their bishop was trying to encourage them by declaring that God would never abandon those who put their trust in Him. "Go to the rampart," he bade a faithful attendant, "and tell me if aid is not at hand." "What did you see?" he asked when the messenger returned. "Nothing," was the reply. A little later the man was sent again, but he had nothing of comfort to report. A third time he climbed the rampart, and now he ran back to the bishop, crying, "A cloud! there is a cloud on the horizon as if made by an army marching!" "It is the aid of God," the bishop exclaimed. "It is the

aid of God," repeated the people, and they fought with fresh courage. The cloud grew larger and larger. Now and then there was a flash of steel or the gleam of a war banner. The bishop was right; it was the brave Roman general Aëtius with his army, and Orleans was saved.

AËTIUS
(Relief on ivory tablet found at Monza, in Northern Italy)

Attila withdrew to the plain of Châlons. The Romans and their former foes, the Goths, had united against him, and on this plain was fought one of the most bloody battles ever known. It raged from the middle of the afternoon until night, and some of the people of the country believed that in the darkness the spirits of those who had fallen arose and kept up the fight in mid-air. Attila retreated across the Rhine. If he had won the day the heathen Huns instead of the Christian Germans would have become the most powerful people of Europe. That is why this conflict at Châlons is counted as one of the decisive battles of the world.

After a winter's rest, Attila started to invade Italy. He meant to go straight to Rome, but the strong city of Aquileia was in his way. After a long siege, however, it yielded. Some of the inhabitants of that and other conquered cities fled to a group of marshy islands, where Venice now stands. City after

14

city he captured and burned. But this wild Hun was not without a sense of humour. While he was strolling through the royal palace in Milan, he came across a picture showing Roman emperors on their thrones with Scythian chiefs kneeling before them and paying them tribute of bags of gold. Attila did not draw the sword of Tyr and cut the picture to fragments; he simply sent for painter and said, "Put those kneeling men upon the thrones, and paint the emperors kneeling to pay tribute."

The Romans were thoroughly frightened, for now Attila was near their city. Aëtius was calm and brave, but he was without troops. Then Pope Leo I., courageous as the Bishop of Orleans, went forth to meet the Huns, and begged Attila to spare the city. Attila yielded, but no one knows why. A legend arose, that the apostles Peter and Paul appeared to him and declared that he should die at once if he did not grant the prayers of Leo. It is certain that before he started for Rome his friends had said to him, "Beware! Remember that Alaric conquered Rome and died." He had no fear of a sword, but he may have been afraid of such warnings as this. Whatever was the reason, he agreed to spare Rome if the Romans would pay him a large ransom.

The gold was paid, and Attila returned to his wooden palace on the Danube. Soon after this he suddenly died. His followers cut off their hair and gashed their faces, so that blood rather than tears might flow for him. His body was enclosed in three coffins, one of gold, one of silver, and one of iron. It was buried at night with a vast amount of treasure.

Then, as in the case of Alaric, the captives who had dug the grave were put to death. His followers belonged to different races. Several chieftains tried to become king, but no one of them was strong enough to hold the tribes together, and they were soon scattered, and the power of the Huns declined forever.

CHAPTER III

GENSERIC THE VANDAL

A FEW years after the death of Attila, Rome was once more in the hands of an invader, Genseric the Vandal. The Vandals were great wanderers. They slowly made their way from the shores of the Baltic Sea to the Danube, passed through what is now France, and went south into Spain. Only eight or nine miles from Spain, just across what is now the Strait of Gibraltar, lay Africa.

Northern Africa belonged to Rome. It was one of her most valued provinces because, while Italy could not raise enough grain to feed her people, Africa could supply all that was needed. Genseric longed to add Africa to his domain, and he was more fortunate than most men who wish to invade a country, for after a little while he received a cordial invitation to come to Africa and bring his soldiers with him. The invitation was given by no less a man than the brave general Boniface, who had been appointed governor of the province. This is the way it came about. Aëtius was jealous of the success of Boniface, and he persuaded the mother of the child emperor to send the governor a letter recalling him.

17

Then he himself wrote a letter to his "friend" Boniface with the warning that the empress was angry with him, and he would lose his head if he risked it in Rome. Boniface was in a hard position. He concluded that the safest thing for him to do was to remain where he was, and ask Genseric to help him to hold Africa.

Genseric did not wait to be urged. He hurried across the Strait of Gibraltar and began his career of violence. A Vandal conquest was more severe than that of any other tribe, for the Vandals seemed to delight in ruining everything that came into their power. They killed men, women, and children; they burned houses and churches; and they destroyed whatever treasures they could not carry away with them. Some said that whenever they conquered a country, they cut down every fruit tree within its limits. This is why people who seem to enjoy spoiling things are sometimes called *vandals*.

After a while Boniface discovered how he had been tricked by Aëtius, and he begged Genseric to leave the country; but the barbarian refused, and Boniface could not drive him away. Genseric and his followers settled in Africa, making the city of Carthage the capital of their kingdom, and they became a nation of pirates. They built light swift vessels and ravaged the shore of any country where they expected to find plunder.

All this time Genseric had his eyes fixed upon Italy, and again he was fortunate enough to be invited to a land which he was longing to invade.

This time the widow of a murdered emperor begged him to come and avenge her wrongs. He wasted no time but crossed the narrow sea and marched up to the walls of Rome. Behold, the gates were flung open, and once more Leo, now a hoary-headed man, came forth with his clergy, all in their priestly robes, to beg the Vandals to have mercy. Genseric made some promises, but they were soon broken. For fourteen days the Vandals did what they would. They were in no hurry; they had plenty of ships to carry away whatever they chose; and after they had chosen, there was little but the walls remaining. They snatched at gold and silver and jewels, of course, but they took also brass, copper, and bronze, silken robes, and even furniture. Works of art were nothing to them unless they were of precious metal and could be melted; and what they did not care to take with them, they broke or burned. The widowed empress had expected to be treated with the greatest honour, but the Vandals stripped off her jewels and threw her and her two daughters on board their ships to be carried to Africa as prisoners.

Genseric kept his nation together as long as he lived; and indeed, though the Romans made many expeditions against the Vandals, it was nearly eighty years before the pirates were conquered.

CHAPTER IV

THE TEUTONS AND THEIR MYTHS

FOR a long while, as we have seen, the Roman Empire had been growing weaker and the Teutons, or Germans, had been growing stronger. These Teutons were a most interesting people. They were tall and strong, with blue eyes and light hair. They were splendid fighters, and nothing made them so happy as the sound of a battle-cry. They cared nothing for wounds, and they felt it a disgrace for any one to meet death quietly at home. A man should die on the field of battle, thought the Teutons; and then one of the Valkyrs, the beautiful war-maidens of Odin, would come and carry him on her swift horse straight to Valhalla, her armour gleaming as she rode through the air, with the flashing glow which men call the northern lights. Valhalla, they believed, was a great hall with shields and spears hanging on its walls. The bravest warriors who had ever fought on the earth were to be found there. Every morning they went out to some glorious battle. At night they came back, their wounds were healed, they drank great cups of mead and

THE RIDE OF THE VALKYRS
H. Hendrich

listened to songs of deeds of valour. Odin, or Woden, king of the gods, ruled in this hall. He had a son Thor, who was sometimes called the thunder-god. Thor rode about in a chariot drawn by goats. He carried with him a mighty hammer, and this he threw at any one who displeased him. Tyr, another son of Odin, whose sword Attila thought he had found, was the god of war.

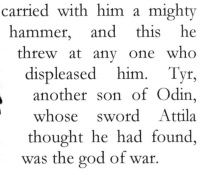

WODEN

Not all the gods were thunderers and fighters. There was Odin's wife, Freya, who ruled the sunshine and the rain, and who loved fairies and flowers and all things dainty and pretty. Then there was Freya's son, Baldur, whom every one loved, and Loki, whom everyone feared and hated. Loki was always getting the gods into trouble, and it was he who brought about the death of Baldur. Freya had once made beasts and birds and trees and everything on the earth that had life promise never to hurt her son; but the mistletoe was so small and harmless that she forgot it. There was a chance for wicked Loki. It was a favourite game of the gods to shoot arrows at Baldur, for they knew that nothing would harm him. One of the gods was blind, and Loki offered to guide his hand, saying that all ought to do honour to so good a god as Baldur. In all innocence, the blind one threw the twig of mistletoe that Loki gave him. Baldur fell down dead, and had to go forever to the land of gloom and darkness.

THOR

The Teutonic story of the creation of the earth was this:—Long ago there was far to the northward a gulf of mist. In the mist was a fountain, and from the fountain there flowed twelve rivers. By and by, the waters of the rivers froze, and then in the north there was nothing but a great mass of ice. Far to the southward was a world of warmth and light. From this a warm wind blew upon the ice and melted it. Clouds were formed, and from them came forth the giant Ymir and his children and his cow. The cow was one day licking the hoar frost and salt from the ice, when she saw the hair of a man. The next day she licked still deeper, and then she saw a man's head. On the third day a living being, strong and beautiful, had taken his place in this strange world. He was a god, and one of his children was

FREYA

Odin. Together the children slew Ymir. Of his body they made the earth, of his blood the seas, of his bones the mountains, of his eyebrows they made Midgard, the mid earth. Odin arranged the seasons, and when the world was covered with green things growing, the gods made man of an ash tree and woman of an alder. An immense ash tree, which grew from the body of Ymir, supported the whole universe. One of its roots extended to Asgard, the home of the gods; one to Jötunheim, the abode of the giants; and one to Niflheim, the region of cold and darkness beneath the earth. It was believed that some day all created things would be destroyed. After this a new heaven and a new earth would be formed in which there would be no wickedness or trouble, and gods and men would live together in peace and happiness. All these fancies had some meaning; for instance, Baldur the beautiful, at sight of whose face all things rejoiced, represented the sunshine.

Poetical as the Germans were in some of their fancies, they were by no means poetical when any fighting was to be done. They had a custom of choosing some man as leader and following him wherever he led; but the moment that he showed himself a poor commander or failed to give them a fair share of whatever spoils they had captured, they left him and sought another chief. When the time had come that the Romans were no longer willing to defend themselves, it seemed to them a most comfortable arrangement to send a messenger to some of the Teuton chiefs to say, "If you will help us in this war, we will give you so much gold." Unluckily for themselves, the Romans looked upon barbarians as nothing more than convenient weapons, and did not stop to think that they were men who kept their eyes open, and who sooner or later would be sure to feel that there was no reason why they, as well as the Romans, should not take what they wanted if they could get it.

A BARBARIAN ALLY OF THE ROMANS
(From the Column of Trajan, at Rome. His weapons are a club and a sword.)

The Goths, especially, were always ready to give up their old ways if they found something better; and by the time Alaric invaded Italy, those who lived nearest the Roman territories had learned something of Christianity, and Ulfilas, a Greek whom they had captured in war, had translated nearly all of the Bible into their language. They had learned to enjoy some of the comforts and conveniences of the Romans. They had discovered that there were better ways of governing a nation than their haphazard fashion of following any one who had won a victory; and they had begun to see that it was a good thing to have established cities. But if they gave up their roving life and made their home in one place, they could no longer live by fishing and hunting, for the rivers and forests would soon be exhausted; they must cultivate the ground. We have seen how the Goths had become the most powerful of all the Teutonic tribes. To so warlike a people, it seemed much easier to take the cultivated ground of the Romans than to make the wild forest land into fields and gardens. These were reasons why the Goths, among all the Germans, were so persistent in their invasions of the Roman Empire. There was one more reason, however, quite as strong as these. It was that other tribes even more barbarous than they were coming from Asia, and pressing upon them in order to get their land. The Romans might have found some way to save their country; but they were too busy enjoying themselves to be troubled about such matters. Their only care seemed to be to find the easiest way out of a difficulty, and when a nation is faced by powerful and determined enemies whose hearts are not set upon a life of ease and luxury, they are sure, sooner or later, to be destroyed.

CHAPTER V

THE STORY OF THE NIBELUNGS

M ANY of the Goths had learned about Christianity, as has been said before; but for a long while most of the Teutons believed, or half believed, in the old fables of gods and heroes. One of these, the story of the Nibelungs, was a special favourite. It was told by father to son for centuries; then some unknown poet put it into poetry. This poem was called the Nibelungen-Lied, or song of the Nibelungs. It began with one of the evil pranks of Loki by which the gallant knight Siegfried became owner of a vast hoard of gold once belonging to a nation of dwarfs called Nibelungs. Siegfried was rich and handsome and brave, and he rode forth into the world, not knowing that the gold was accursed and would bring trouble to whoever might own it.

His first adventure was in Isenland, or Iceland, where he broke through a magic ring of fire that for many years had burned around a lofty castle on the summit of a mountain. In this castle lay Brunhild, a disobedient Valkyr whom Odin had punished by putting her and the king and court who had received her into a sleep. This was to last till some hero should pass the ring of fire. Siegfried broke through, found the beautiful maiden, and became betrothed to her. But after a brief period of happiness Odin bade the hero leave Isenland and go elsewhere in search of adventures.

Siegfried went next to the land of Burgundy, and there he found a new exploit awaiting him. King Günther had heard of the beautiful Brunhild, and was eager to marry her. Many a man had lost his life because of this same wish; for whoever would win her must outdo her in the games, and if he failed, both he and his attendant knights were put to death. The king and Siegfried set off for Isenland, and the games began. First, Brunhild threw her heavy javelin against the king's shield; but Günther cast it back at her so powerfully that she fell to the ground. When she rose, she caught up a stone, so heavy that twelve knights could hardly lift it, and hurled it an amazing distance. Then at one leap she sprang to where the stone had fallen; but Günther threw the stone farther and leaped farther. Then the Valkyr yielded and became his wife. She did not guess that it was not Günther who had beaten her, but Siegfried. Siegfried had a magic cap of darkness, and when he put it on, he became invisible; so while Günther went through the motions, it was really Siegfried who threw the javelin and hurled the stone and even carried Günther in his arms far beyond the leap of the Valkyr. So it was that Brunhild became the wife of Günther. As for Siegfried, an enchantment had been thrown about him, and he had entirely forgotten that he had ever ridden through the ring of fire or seen Brunhild before. The hand of the king's sister, the gentle, lovely Kriemhild, was to be his reward for his service to King Günther; and now both weddings were celebrated. Günther and Brunhild remained in Burgundy, and Siegfried carried Kriemhild to his kingdom in the Jutland.

SIEGFRIED FIGHTING THE DRAGON

Even if Siegfried had forgotten Brunhild, she had not forgotten him, and she meant to have her revenge. She persuaded Günther to invite Siegfried and Kriemhild to Burgundy. It was easy for a quarrel to arise between the two queens, and Hagen, uncle of Kriemhild, took the part of Brunhild. He pretended that war had arisen against Günther, and Siegfried agreed to fight for his host. Kriemhild begged her uncle to help Siegfried whenever he was in peril; and the treacherous Hagen replied, "Surely; but first tell me where his chief peril lies. Is there some one way by which he may most easily lose his life?" "Yes," answered Kriemhild, "he once slew a dragon and bathed himself in its blood. Therefore no weapon can harm him save in one tiny place between his shoulders which was not touched by the blood because it was covered by a linden leaf." "Then do you sew a mark upon his garment directly over that place," said the false Hagen, "that I may guard it well." One day Siegfried went out hunting with Günther and Hagen, and it was not long before his body was brought back to the sorrowing Kriemhild. The treachery of Hagen, however, was not to be hidden, for during the funeral rites Siegfried's wounds began to bleed afresh as Hagen passed the bier; and from this Kriemhild knew that he was the murderer of her husband.

Siegfried's father lovingly begged Kriemhild to return to the Jutland with him; but she would not leave Burgundy, for she hoped some day to avenge her murdered husband. She sent for the Nibelung treasure and gave generously to all around her. Then wicked Hagen began to fear that the hearts of the people would turn towards her. Therefore he stole the treasure and sank it deep in the river Rhine; but he meant to recover it some day for himself.

It came about that King Etzel of Hungary sent a noble envoy to beg for the hand of the widowed queen. She answered him kindly, for she said to herself, "Etzel is brave and powerful, and if I wed him, I may be able some day to avenge my Siegfried." So it was that Kriemhild became the wife of Etzel, and was true and faithful to him for thirteen years. At the end of that time she asked him to invite the king and court of Burgundy to visit them. The Burgundians accepted the invitation, though the murderer Hagen urged them to remain at home. In

BRINGING BACK THE BODY OF SIEGFRIED
H. Hendrich

Hungary they were treated with all courtesy; but Kriemhild had told her wrongs to her Hungarian friends, and as the guests sat at a magnificent feast given in their honour, the Hungarian knights dashed into the hall of feasting, and slew almost every one. Günther and Hagen yet lived, and Kriemhild bade Hagen reveal where he had hidden her stolen treasure. "Never, so long as Günther lives," was his reply.

Kriemhild ordered Günther to be put to death and his head taken to Hagen, but Hagen still refused to tell what had become of the treasure. In her anger

HAGEN THROWS THE NIBELUNGEN TREASURE
INTO THE RHINE
(From a fresco in the Royal Palace, Munich)

Kriemhild caught up the magic sword of Siegfried and struck off Hagen's head at a blow. Then one of the Burgundians cried, "Whatever may become of me, she shall gain nothing by this murderous deed"; and in a moment he had run her through with his sword. So ended the story of the treasure of the Nibelungs, which brought ill to every one who possessed it.

CHAPTER VI

CLOVIS

OF all the Teutons who came to live on Roman territory, the most important were the Franks, or free men. They had no wish to wander over the world when they had once found a country that pleased them, and so, since they liked the land about the mouth of the Rhine, they settled there and held on to it, adding more and more wherever a little fighting would win it for them. Each tribe had its chief; but Clovis, one of these chiefs, came at last to rule them all. The country west of the Rhine, then called Gaul, was still partly held by the Romans, but Clovis meant to drive them away and keep the land for the Franks. When he was only twenty-one, he led his men against

BRONZE HELMET OF A FRANKISH WARRIOR
(Found near the river Seine in France. Now in the Louvre, Paris)

the Roman governor at Soissons and took the place. From here he sent out expeditions to conquer one bit of land after another and to bring back rich booty. The most valuable treasures were usually kept in the churches, and the heathen Franks took great delight in seizing these. Among the church treasures captured at Rheims was a marvellously beautiful vase. Now the bishop of Rheims was on good terms with Clovis, and he sent a messenger to the young chief to beg that, even if the soldiers would not return all the holy vessels of the church, this one at least might be given back. Clovis bade the messenger follow on to Soissons, where the booty would be divided.

At Soissons, when all the warriors were assembled, the king pointed to the vase and said, "I ask you, O most valiant warriors, not to refuse to me the vase in addition to my rightful part." Most of the

FRANKISH
COSTUME
OF THE
TIME OF
CLOVIS
(From an illus-
tration in an
old Bible at
Rome)

soldiers were wise enough not to object to the wishes of so powerful a chief; but one foolish, envious man swung his battle-axe and crushed the vase, crying, "Thou shalt receive nothing of this unless a just lot gives it to thee." It is no wonder that the whole army were amazed at such audacity. Clovis said nothing, but quietly handed the crushed vase to the bishop's messenger. He did not forget the insult, however, and a year later, when he was reviewing his troops, he declared that this man's weapons were not in fit condition, and with one blow of his axe he struck the soldier dead, saying, "Thus thou didst to the vase at Soissons."

Clovis showed himself so much stronger than the other chiefs of the Franks that at length they all accepted him as their king. Soon after this, he began to think about taking a wife. The story of his wooing is almost like a fairy tale. In the land of Burgundy lived a fair young girl named Clotilda, whose wicked uncle had slain her father, mother, and brothers that he might get the kingdom. Clovis had heard how beautiful and good she was, and he sent an envoy to ask for her hand in marriage. The wicked uncle was afraid to have her marry so powerful a ruler, lest she should avenge the slaughter of her family; but he did not dare to refuse Clovis or to murder the girl after Clovis had asked that she might become his queen. There was nothing to do but to send her to the king of the Franks. Clovis was delighted with her, and they were married with all festivities.

Clotilda was a Christian, and she was much grieved that her husband should remain a heathen. She told him many times about her God, but nothing moved him. When their first child was born, Clotilda had the baby baptized. Not long afterwards, the little boy grew ill and died. "That is because he was baptized in the name of your God," declared Clovis bitterly. "If he had been consecrated in the name of my gods, he would be alive still." Nevertheless, when a second son was born, Clotilda had him baptized. He, too, fell ill, and the king said, "He was baptized in the name of Christ, and he will soon die." But the mother prayed to God, and by God's will the boy recovered. Still Clovis would not give up the gods of his fathers. It came to pass, however, that he was engaged in a fierce battle near where

Cologne now stands. His enemies were fast getting the better of him, and he was almost in despair, when suddenly he thought of the God of his queen, and he cried, "Jesus Christ, whom Clotilda declares to be the Son of the living God, if Thou wilt grant me victory over these enemies, I will believe in Thee and be baptized in Thy name." Soon the enemy fled, and Clovis did not doubt that his prayer had been answered.

When he told Clotilda of this, she was delighted. She sent for the bishop and asked him to teach her husband the true religion. After a little, Clovis said to him, "I am glad to listen to you, but my people will not leave their gods." He thought a while and then he declared, "I will go forth and tell them what you have told me." He went out among his people, and, as the legend says, even before he had spoken a word, the people cried out all together, "We are ready to follow the immortal God." Then the bishop ordered the font to be prepared for the baptism of the king. The procession set out from the palace and passed through streets made gorgeous with embroidered hangings. First came the clergy, chanting hymns as they marched, and bearing the Gospels and a golden cross. After them walked the bishop, leading the king by the hand. Behind them came the queen, and after her the people. They passed through the door and into the church. The candles gleamed, the house was hung with tapestries of the purest white and was fragrant with incense; and there the king of the Franks, his sisters, and more than three thousand of his warriors, besides a

BAPTISM OF CLOVIS

throng of women and children, were baptized and marked with the sign of the cross.

The times were harsh and rude, and even a king who was looked upon as a Christian ruler never dreamed of hesitating to do many cruel deeds. Clovis wished to enlarge his kingdom, and he could always find some excuse for attacking any tribe living on land next his own. He cared nothing for his word, and to get what he wanted, he was ready to lie or steal or murder.

Clovis died in 511, but before that time all the lands between the lower Rhine and the Pyrenees had been obliged to acknowledge his rule. He made Paris his capital, and went there to live. This was the beginning of France. The descendants of Clovis held the throne for nearly two centuries and a half. They were called Merovingians from Merovæus, the grandfather of Clovis.

CHAPTER VII

THEODORIC THE OSTROGOTH

IN 476, one year before the death of Genseric the Vandal, a Goth named Odoacer became ruler of Italy. He had taken the throne from the handsome boy who had been ruling as Emperor, permitting him to escape and allowing him six thousand gold pieces a year. The Roman Senate, which had once been a courageous and patriotic body of men, decided that there was no longer any Western Empire, and that its rule belonged to the Emperor in the East, whose capital was Constantinople. The Emperor accepted this view, and left Odoacer in Italy to represent him. This event is called the fall of the Western Empire.

In this same year, 476, Theodoric became king of the Ostrogoths, or Goths of the East. The Emperor in the East had hired this nation to defend the lower Danube, and Theodoric, a little boy of the royal family, had been sent to Constantinople as a hostage, or pledge that his people would keep their promises. When Theodoric grew up and became king, the Emperor permitted him to go and drive Odoacer out of Italy. Theodoric started with his army, and with all the rest of his tribe, for they meant not only to drive out Odoacer, but to make their homes in Italy.

There were three fierce battles. Finally it was agreed that Odoacer and Theodoric should rule with equal powers. Before long, however, Theodoric

treacherously murdered Odoacer and became sole ruler of Italy. He meant to rule like the Romans, but more wisely. He chose from the old Roman laws those which he thought just. He broke up the vast estates of the very wealthy and made many small farms, so that much more grain was raised. He built many handsome buildings, and he encouraged his subjects to read and study. The emperors in the East were doing their best to keep back the hordes of Huns and other barbarians, and it began to seem as if Italy would grow into a powerful, well-governed country with Goths for its rulers.

REMAINS OF THE
PALACE OF
THEODORIC AT
RAVENNA, ITALY

(This city rose to great
splendour under the
rule of Theodoric)

That might have come to pass if a brilliant man named Justinian had not become ruler in the Eastern Empire after the death of Theodoric. His great wish was to bring back Italy and Africa to the Empire. Fortunately for him, he had an officer named Belisarius, who was not only a skilful general, but who had the power of making his soldiers eager to follow him. Under his lead, Italy and Africa were regained, the Vandals in Africa were scattered, and the Goths in Italy were hopelessly beaten. Justinian brought together all that was known of the Roman law, and it is upon his Code of Laws that the governments of the chief countries of Europe are founded. While he lived, there seemed some hope that the Empire would be mighty again; but as soon as he died, it lapsed into the same weak, tottering state as just before his day.

CHAPTER VIII

CHARLES MARTEL

WHEN King Clovis died, his four sons divided the kingdom among them much as if it had been a farm. Then they quarrelled, and a quarrel in those days led to savage fighting. Each ruler intended to get as much as he could, and if any one stood in the way the first thought was, "Kill him." For instance, one of Clovis's sons died, leaving three boys. Queen Clotilda tried to protect the rights of her grandchildren, but two of her sons sent her a sword and a pair of scissors. That meant, "Should you rather have the boys slain or have them lose their long hair?" To lose their long hair would shut them out of the royal family, and Clotilda replied that she would rather see them dead than disgraced. Two of the boys were at once murdered by their uncle.

For more than a century, the Frankish kingdom was full of quarrels and fighting. During the following century, a king was always on the throne, but he never ruled; and these sovereigns have been nicknamed the "do-nothing kings." The real rulers were officers called mayors of the palace. The

42

"mayor" was at first only a sort of royal attendant, but several of the kings were children when they came to the throne; and the mayors acted as their guardians but without all the regal powers. Some of the kings were stupid, and some cared only for amusement, and hardly any of them were strong and manly enough to govern. The mayors of the palace were rulers in peace, and as the "do-nothing kings" were of course unable to lead armies, the mayors became also commanders in war. This arrangement suited the Frankish nobles. They were always afraid that their kings would get too much power over them; but as a mayor was chosen from among themselves, they were not jealous of his power.

One of these mayors was named Pepin. He treated the king with the utmost respect, permitted him to live on one of the royal estates, and sent servants to wait on him. When some national festival was to be held, the king was brought to court dressed in most elegant robes and with his long hair floating over his shoulders. He rode in a heavy wagon drawn by oxen and driven by a cowherd. This was according to the ancient custom, and the people would have been displeased to have it altered. He was escorted into the palace and seated upon the throne, and the nobles came to do him honour. He recited a little speech, composed for him beforehand, urging the army to be valiant and to be always ready for service. If ambassadors were to be received, he met them graciously, and said what Mayor Pepin told him to say. Then with all deference he was led to the cart and driven back to the estate upon which he lived. He was free to go on hunting or raising doves or combing his long hair until a figurehead was needed again.

When Pepin died, his son Charles became mayor. It was fortunate that he was a good fighter, for there was a great deal of fighting to be done. There were hostile tribes on the north and east to be subdued. Then, too, there were rumors of trouble coming from another people, the Mohammedans. It was essential that Charles should have an army ready to set out at a moment's notice. But he could not keep an army without the help of the nobles, and for such help he must pay, and pay well. The churches owned a vast amount of land and money; and when Charles needed either to reward the nobles, he took it. It is probable that he did not give away the land, but only lent it to his nobles by what is called a feudal tenure; that is, so long as a noble provided a certain number of men for the mayor's army, he might hold the land and get as much gain from it as he could. This was all very well for the nobles, but it is no wonder that the bishops were not pleased. And the army so maintained was to be used to defend them against the Mohammedans.

The history of these people is interesting. About one hundred and sixty years before that time, a man named Mohammed was born in Mecca in Arabia, and he became so famous when a man that the people who knew him as a child fancied that many wonderful things had happened to him when he was small. It was said that the sheep bowed to him as he passed by, and that even the moon stooped from her place in the heavens to do him honour. While he was in the house of his nurse, so the legend says, her well never dried and her pastures were always fresh and green.

The little boy soon lost both father and mother, and was brought up in the house of his uncle. He must have been a most lovable boy, for every one seems to have been kind to him. This uncle held an office of great honour,—he was guardian of a certain black stone which, it was said, the angel Gabriel had given to Abraham. The stone was built into the outer wall of the Kaaba, a little square temple which the Arabians looked upon as especially holy. Most of them were worshipers of idols, and the Kaaba was the home of enough idols to provide a different one for every day in the year. Throngs of pilgrims journeyed to Mecca to kiss the stone and worship in the Kaaba; and the boy must have heard marvellous tales of the strange places from which they came. His uncle was a merchant and used to go with caravans to Syria and elsewhere to buy and sell goods. When Mohammed was twelve years old, he begged earnestly to be allowed to go with him. The uncle said "No." Then the boy pleaded, "But, my uncle, who will take care of me when you are gone?" The tender-hearted man could not refuse any longer, and Mohammed went on his first journey.

After this, he always travelled with his uncle, and when the uncle went out to help his tribe fight another, he became the uncle's armour-bearer. He learned about life in a caravan, and about buying and selling goods, and while he was hardly more than a boy, he was often employed by merchants to go on such trips as their agent. At length he was engaged by a wealthy widow named Kadijah to manage the large business which the death of her husband had left in her charge. She became more and more pleased with the young man, and after a while she sent a trusty slave to offer him her hand. He was surprised, but not at all unwilling, and soon there was a generous wedding feast with music and dancing. The house was open to all who chose to come, and a camel was killed that its flesh might be given to the poor.

Mohammed thought much about religious questions. He came to believe that his people were wrong in worshipping idols, and that there was only one true God. He used to go to a cavern a few miles from Mecca to pray and meditate. One month in every year he gave up entirely to this. After a while, he began to have strange dreams and visions. In one of these he thought the angel Gabriel held before him a silken cloth on which there was golden writing and bade him read it. "But I do not know how to read," replied Mohammed. "Read, in the name of the Most High," said the angel; and suddenly the power to read the letters came to him, and he found the writings were commands of God. Then the angel declared, "Thou art the prophet of God."

Mohammed told Kadijah of his vision, and she believed that the angel had really come to him. After a little, he began to preach wherever people would listen. A few believed in him, but most people only laughed at his story. Still he kept on preaching,

THE VISION OF MOHAMMED

and after a while, although he had but few followers in Mecca, there were many in Medina who had come to believe that he was the prophet of God. He decided that it was best for him to go to them, and in the year 622 he and a few friends escaped from their enemies in Mecca and went to Medina. This is called the Hegira, or flight. To this day Mohammedans do not count the years from the birth of Christ, but from the Hegira.

As soon as the prophet was in Medina, his followers began to build a mosque, or place for prayer, in which he might preach. They made the walls of earth and brick. The pillars were the trunks of palm trees, and the roof was formed of their branches with a thatch of leaves. He decided that his disciples should be called to prayer five times a day, and after all these centuries the call, or muezzin, is still heard in the East from some minaret of each mosque,— "God is great. There is no God but God. Mohammed is the apostle of God. Come to prayers. Come to prayers." At dawn the crier adds, "Prayer is better than sleep." Every true Mussulman, as followers of Mohammed are called, is bound to obey this rule of prayer, and as he prays, he must turn his face toward Mecca. He is also commanded to make at least one pilgrimage to Mecca before he dies, and to kiss the sacred black stone. It is still in the wall of the Kaaba, but the Kaaba itself is now within a mosque so large that it will hold 35,000 persons.

It is probable that Mohammed never learned to read or write, but his followers jotted down his words on bits of palm leaves or skins or even the shoulder-blades of animals, and many of them they learned by heart. After the death of the prophet, the caliphs, as his successors were called, collected these sayings and arranged them in a book called the Koran, which is the sacred volume of the Mussulmans.

CAPTURE OF MECCA BY MOHAMMED

For a long while, Mohammed preached peace and gentleness and charity, and he won many followers. Then he came to believe that if people would not obey his teachings, it was right to make war upon them. He marched against Mecca with a large army of his disciples, and soon captured it. After a time, either by preaching or by fighting, the Mohammedans, or Mussulmans, became the rulers of all Arabia. After the death of their prophet, they continued their conquests. They overcame Syria, Persia, Egypt, northern Africa, and Spain. A little later they swarmed over the Pyrenees, and pushed on as far north as Tours. In 732, just one hundred years after the death of Mohammed, the Mohammedans met the Frankish army of Charles on the plain of Tours, and after a terrible combat the Mohammedans were so completely overwhelmed that they retreated toward Spain and never again tried to conquer the land of the Franks.

It was fortunate for all Europe that the Frankish troops were led by so valiant a warrior as Charles. He not only led, but he fought with his own hands; and he swung his mighty battle-axe with such crushing blows that after this battle he was known as Charles the Hammer, or Charles Martel. It was no wonder that when the long-haired Merovingian died who was then called king of the Franks, none saw need of putting another on the throne while Charles lived.

When Charles Martel died, his son Pepin became mayor. He is known as Pepin the Short. By this time, the Pope had become so powerful that kings liked to have his sanction to whatever they proposed to do. Before long, Pepin sent an embassy to him to say, "Who ought to be king, the man who has the name or the man who has the power?" The Pope thought it reasonable that the man who

CHARLES MARTEL IN THE BATTLE OF TOURS.

was really king should also be king in name; and so it came to pass that no more Merovingians drove up from their farms once a year to sit on the throne for a day. Pepin was made king, and soon the Pope travelled all the way from Rome to St. Denis near Paris, to crown the new sovereign and anoint him with the sacred oil. He was the first king of the Carolingian Line.

CHAPTER IX

CHARLEMAGNE

P EPIN THE SHORT had done a great deal to unite the kingdom; but when he died, he left it to his two sons, and so divided it again. The older son died in a few years; and now the kingdom of the Franks was in the hands of Charlemagne, if he could hold it. First came trouble with the Saxons who lived about the lower Rhine and the Elbe. They and the Franks were both Germans, but the Franks had had much to do with the Romans, and had learned many of their ways. Missionaries, too, had dwelt among them and had taught them Christianity, while the Saxons were still heathen. It was fully thirty years before the Saxons were subdued. During those years, Charlemagne watched them closely. He fought, to be sure, whenever they rebelled, and he made some severe laws and saw to it that these were obeyed. More than this, however, he sent missionaries to them, and he built churches. He carried away many Saxon boys as hostages. These boys were carefully brought up and were taught Christianity. They learned to like the Frankish ways of living, and when they had grown up and were sent home, they urged their friends to yield and become peaceful subjects of the great king; and finally the land of the Saxons became a part of the Frankish kingdom.

Charlemagne had only begun the Saxon war, when the Pope asked for help against the Lombards, a tribe of Teutons who had settled in Northern Italy. The king was quite ready to give it, for he, too, had a quarrel with them; and in a year or two their ruler had been shut up in a monastery and Charlemagne had been crowned with the old iron crown of Lombardy.

This war had hardly come to an end before the king led his troops into Spain against the Mohammedans. There, too, he was successful; but at Roncesvalles he lost a favourite follower, Count Roland. Roland and the warriors who perished with him were so young and brave that the Franks never wearied of recounting their noble deeds. Later the story was put into a fine poem, called the "Song of Roland," which long afterward men sang as they dashed into battle.

In the year 800, a great honour was shown to Charlemagne, for as he was kneeling at the altar in Rome on Christmas Day, the Pope set a crown upon his head, and the people cried, "Long life and victory to the mighty Charles, the great and pacific Emperor of the Romans, crowned of God!" Charlemagne was now not only king of the Franks, but Roman Emperor. This empire, however, was smaller than it had been in the earlier days, for it included now only France, part of Germany and of Italy, and a little

COUNT ROLAND AT RONCESVALLES
Evelyn Paul

strip at the north of Spain.

Charlemagne had become a great ruler, and other rulers were anxious to win his friendship. Haroun-al-Rashid, or *Harun the Just*, the Caliph of Bagdad, hero of *The Arabian Nights*, was one of his special friends. This caliph was a poet and learned man. He founded schools throughout his kingdom in which medicine, geometry, and astronomy might be studied. Charlemagne did not write poetry, but he was a close student, and he desired the boys of his kingdom to be educated. One of his orders reads, "Let every monastery and every abbey have its school, where boys may be taught the Psalms, the system of musical notation, singing, arithmetic, and grammar, and let the books which are given them be free from faults, and let care be taken that the boys do not spoil them either when reading or writing." When he returned from one of his campaigns, he sent for a group of schoolboys and bade them show him their work. The boys from the poorer families had done their best, and he thanked them heartily. "Try now to reach perfection," he said, "and you shall be highly honoured in my sight." The sons of the nobles had thought that as their fathers were rich and of high rank there was no need of their working, and they had nothing good to show their king. He burst out upon them in anger, "You pretty and dainty little gentlemen who count upon your birth and your wealth, you have disregarded my orders and your own reputations and neglected your stud-ies. Let me promise you this: If you do not make haste to make good your former negligence, never think to get any favours from Karl."

CORONATION OF CHARLEMAGNE

As there were few learned men in the Frankish kingdom, the king sent to scholars in other parts of Europe and offered them generous rewards to come to the Franks as their teachers. He collected a library and established a school at his own court; and there the mighty Emperor, his family, and his courtiers, gathered around some wise man and learned of him. The Emperor was interested in everything. He often got up in the night to study the stars. Once when the planet Mars could not be seen, he wrote to his teacher, "What do you think of this Mars? Is it the influence of the sun? Is it a miracle ? Could he have been two years about performing the course of a single one?"

Charlemagne was a tall, large, dignified man. On state occasions he dressed most splendidly, but at other times he wore simple clothes and liked best those that were ornamented with the work of his wife and daughters. He was an expert horseman and swimmer, and he taught his sons to ride and to use the sword and the spear. He took charge of his own farms, he built churches and bridges, and he began a canal to connect the Rhine with the Danube. He encouraged trade, making the taxes upon merchants as light as possible. He collected the ancient German songs, he had a grammar of the language written, he improved the singing in the churches, and he even had the coinage of the kingdom manufactured in his own palace. All this was in addition to the fifty or more campaigns that he was obliged to make. Surely he was the busiest of monarchs and the busiest of Germans; for, although the land of the Franks is now France, yet it must not be forgotten that the Franks were German, and that the German "Karl der Grosse," would be a better name for the great ruler than the French "Charlemagne."

When the mighty Emperor died, his empire fell to his son, a gentle, kindly man, but not strong enough to meet the lawless chiefs who opposed him. He was followed by his three sons; and again the vast empire was divided. The sons were not satisfied, and they went to war. After much fighting, a treaty

THE EMPEROR CHARLEMAGNE
From a Portrait in Nürnberg Museum

was made at Verdun in 843. The eldest son, Lothair, received the title of Emperor. His part of the domain was northern Italy and a broad strip of land extending to the North Sea. The kingdom of the youngest lay to the east of this, and that of the second son, Charles the Bald, to the west. Charles the Bald held more than half of what is now called France, and it is from this treaty and the reign of Charles that the French count the beginning of the kingdom of France.

CHAPTER X

THE COMING OF THE TEUTONS TO ENGLAND

THE Celts, as has been said before, left their old home in Asia in very early times and moved slowly across Europe. At length they came to the ocean. The tribes behind were pressing upon them, and the Celts were not to be stopped by so narrow a body of water as the English Channel. Many of them crossed to Britain. There they lived in small huts made of poles fastened together at the top. They knew how to make boats with planks and nails, but oftener they made them by covering wicker frameworks with skins. Their priests were called Druids, and it is thought that the great stones at Stonehenge, on Salisbury Plain, are the remains of rude temples in which sacrifices were offered. These Celts, or Britons, painted their bodies blue, for they thought this would make them seem more terrible to their enemies. Rough as they were, they were fond of pretty things, and they made themselves bracelets and necklaces of gold. Those who lived inland were savage, but those who dwelt nearest to the Continent were somewhat civilized. They raised wheat and barley and kept many cattle. They had no towns, but gathered in little villages.

STONEHENGE
(In the middle is a slab called the altar. This was originally surrounded by circles of stone posts connected by slabs resting on their tops)

This is the way the Britons lived when the Romans came upon them. The Romans were always ready to conquer a new country; and they meant to subdue Britain, or Albion, as it was then called. They obliged the Britons in the greater part of England to obey them; but they were unable to subdue the savage tribes of the northern part of the island; and finally, to keep them from raiding the land which they ruled, they built two great walls with watchtowers and strongholds across the country. Some of the Teutons on the Continent were also troublesome, and therefore the Romans erected a line of forts around the south-eastern shore of England. These Romans were famous road-makers, and they built excellent highways, some of which exist to this day. They made settlements; they erected handsome town houses and country houses with statues and vases and pavements of many-coloured marble, and they built many of their famous baths. The Romans were the rulers, and the Britons had to obey. It is probable that many of the Britons were obliged to enter the Roman army, and that many of those who did not become soldiers were treated as slaves.

LANDING OF THE ROMANS IN BRITAIN.

The Romans could have conquered the troublesome northern tribes, but as we have seen, the Goths were pressing upon the boundaries of their empire, and Alaric had invaded Italy and plundered

Rome itself. Every soldier in the Roman army was now needed to help protect the empire, and so officers and men sailed away from the British shores and left the people to take care of themselves.

ROMAN BATHS
(At Bath, an English watering-place noted for its hot springs. Its Roman name was "Baths of the Sun")

The Britons were better able to do this before the coming of the Romans. They were excellent fighters, but they had become so used to being led by Roman officers that when left alone they were helpless.

The savages were coming down upon them from the north, and the three tribes of Teutons, the Saxons, Angles, and Jutes, were threatening them from the region between the Baltic and the North Sea. The Britons could not protect themselves, and they sent a pitiful appeal to the Roman commander Aëtius to come and help them. "The barbarians," it said, "drive us to the sea, and the sea drives us back to the barbarians; and between them we are either slain or drowned." Aëtius, however, was too busy trying to keep other barbari-

ANCIENT JUTISH BOAT
(It was found some years ago buried in a peat bog in South Jutland, so perfectly preserved that the parts could be put together)

ans from Rome to help people so far away as England, and he could do nothing for them. The Britons believed that of all their enemies the Teutons were the strongest; and they decided to ask them to come to Britain and help drive away the others. They might have the island of Thanet for their home, the Britons promised.

The Jutes came first, under the two brothers, Hengist and Horsa, it is said; and they were followed by the Angles and Saxons. These Teutons helped to drive away the other tribes, according to the bargain; but soon they found Thanet too small for them, and so, just as one tribe had been driving another to the westward for centuries, they drove the Britons to the westward. Some Britons were killed, some became slaves, and some hid away in the mountains of Western England. The Teutons called these Wealh, or Welsh, that is, strangers or foreigners; and it is from this that the country of Wales takes its name.

The Britons were not conquered all at once by any means, for they fought most courageously, and it was many years before the Teutons became masters of the entire country. The Angles scattered so widely throughout the land that it took its name from them and became known as the land of the Angles, or Angle-land, and finally England. The Saxons, however, were strongest of the three peoples, and therefore their name is generally given to all the invaders. Their descendants take both names and are known as Anglo-Saxons.

SAINT GREGORY AND THE ENGLISH SLAVE CHILDREN.

The Britons had become Christians long before the coming of the Saxons, but the Saxons were heathen. After these savage invaders had been in England about a century, some young people of their race were sold in Rome as slaves. They had golden hair and blue eyes, and to a saintly monk named Gregory who was passing through the market-place they seemed exceedingly beautiful. "Who are they?" he asked. The answer was, "Angli," that is, *Angles*. He declared that they would be *not Angles but angels*, if they were Christians. Gregory never lost his interest in the Angles, and if he had been permitted, he would gladly have gone to England as a missionary. After some years he became Pope Gregory the Great, and then, although he himself could not go, he sent Saint Augustine to preach to them. The king of Kent had a Christian wife, and therefore Saint Augustine went first to him and asked if he might tell him about the religion of Christ. The king was willing to hear him, but not in a house, for if there was any magic about this new faith, he thought the evil spirits would have far less power in the open air. He listened closely, and then he went home to think over what he had heard. After a while he told Saint Augustine that he believed the Christian faith was true. This teaching spread over England, and soon the country was no longer heathen.

CHAPTER XI

THE STORY OF BEOWULF

THE SAXONS were fond of singing at their feasts old songs about a hero named Beowulf. Those of them who left their earlier home and came to England did not forget these songs. More incidents were added, and by and by, just as in the case of the tale of the Nibelungs and that of King Arthur, some one wove them together into one long story. The following is the story of "Beowulf."

The old king Hrothgar, who ruled in the land of the Danes, built a mighty hall in which his heroes might feast when they returned from their hard-fought battles. Every one who saw it admired it, but a wicked monster called Grendel, who prowled about in the darkness, was angry. He could not bear to hear the merry sounds of music and feasting; and one night while the men lay asleep, he crept up to the hall and slew thirty of the warriors, dragging their bodies away with him to devour.

Night after night this same slaughter went on,

THE WICKED MONSTER GRENDEL
J. H. F. Bacon, A. R. A.

and the old king was almost broken-hearted at the loss of his beloved heroes. But help was coming. The young champion Beowulf, of the land of Gotland, had heard of the trouble, and he determined to free the king and his men. So, with some brave comrades, he sailed away from his home, and soon reached the land of the Danes. The young warriors

had hardly stepped on shore when the warden of the land, who had been watching them from the cliffs, demanded sharply who they were, for he feared they might be enemies. Upon learning Beowulf's name and the purpose for which he had come, he conducted the strangers to the hall of Hrothgar. Then the king was glad at heart, for he had heard of the amazing prowess of Beowulf.

THE ARRIVAL OF
BEOWULF IN
HROTHGAR'S REALM

That night, while the warriors lay asleep, Grendel stole up through the mists, as usual. His eyes shone like fire as he stretched out his arm to seize the newcomer. But Beowulf caught his hand and held it in such a grip as the monster had never known. He was afraid and tried to flee, but he could not. The heroes awoke and drew their swords, but no weapon could pierce the skin of Grendel; he must be overcome by strength alone. At length he escaped, but his arm was torn from its socket and left in the iron grasp of Beowulf.

In the morning there was great rejoicing. The king loaded the hero with lavish gifts. The queen brought him handsome garments and hung about his neck a fair golden collar; and all were glad and happy.

Alas, on the following night Grendel's mother, another monster as terrible as he, came up from her cavern, beneath a lake, for revenge. She seized and carried away with her one who was very dear to the aged Hrothgar. The king grieved sorely, but Beowulf promised vengeance. Then Beowulf and Hrothgar and a company of chosen men found their way by a lonely path to the lake in which was the den of the fiends. The head of him who was dear to Hrothgar lay on a rock, and swimming in the water were fearful serpents and dragons. Beowulf put on his armour and sprang into the lake. Down, down he sank through the gloomy water. Grendel's mother clutched at him and dragged him into her frightful den. The men by the shore saw the water become red with blood and they grew very sorrowful; but after a long, long while they saw Beowulf swimming toward the land. He had slain Grendel's mother, and he bore with him the terrible head of Grendel.

Then there was great joy in the beautiful hall of King Hrothgar. Many costly gifts were bestowed upon him who had delivered the followers of the king, and then Beowulf bade them all farewell and set out for his homeland.

Beowulf was soon chosen chief of his people and ruled for many years. When he was an old man, a fire-breathing dragon that dwelt in his country came forth by night and went through the land killing people and burning towns and cities. This dragon guarded a vast treasure, and King Beowulf said to himself, "I will win this treasure for my people, and I will avenge their wrongs." He did slay the dragon, but he himself was mortally wounded.

His men grieved sorely. They built a great funeral pyre, all hung about with helmets and shields and coats of mail, and on it they laid gently the body of their dead leader. Afterward they reared in his honour a mighty mound on a hill beside the sea, and in it they buried many rings of gold and other treasures which they had brought forth from the dragon's cave. In after days they often spoke together of Beowulf, and they said, "He cared more for glory than did any other king who dwelt on the earth. He was kind and gentle, too, and he truly loved his people."

CHAPTER XII

SAINT PATRICK

A FEW years before Alaric invaded Italy, a boy was born in Britain, probably on the western coast, who was to become the famous Saint Patrick. It was a wild, rude country. There were bears and wolves and wild boars. It was damp and cold; there was much fog and little sunshine. There were worse troubles than a disagreeable climate, for pirates from Ireland or Caledonia some-times dashed up to the shore, made savage forays into the country, and sailed away with bands of captives to be sold as slaves. This fate befell Patrick when a boy of about sixteen. For several years, he was a slave in Ireland and spent much of his time tending cattle. He had been brought up as a Christian, and as he watched his cattle on the hills, he prayed, some days a hundred times. At length there was a chance to escape,

SAINT
PATRICK

and he fled to his home. All his kindred welcomed him and begged him, now that he was rescued from such great dangers, never to go away.

Still his heart was with the Irish. He dreamt one night that a man held before him a letter which began, "The Voice of the Irish;" and as he read, he seemed to hear the people who dwelt by the western ocean calling, "Come and dwell with us," and he

made up his mind to spend his life preaching to them.

When the time had come that he felt himself prepared, he returned to the island where he had been a captive. Other preachers went with him, and they travelled up and down the land, telling the people every

BELL OF
ST. PATRICK
(About 14½
inches high)

where of the religion of Christ. They wore sandals, and a sort of long cloak which was no more than a large round piece of cloth with a hole in the middle to put the head through. The fore part of their heads was shaved, and the rest of their hair hung down upon their shoulders. When they went on long journeys, they rode in clumsy, two-wheeled wagons; but if the journeys were short, they travelled on foot, staff in hand, chanting psalms as they

SHRINE OF ST.
PATRICK'S BELL.

walked. They carried mass-books and copies of the Gospels and portable altars, and bells made by riveting two pieces of sheet iron together into the form of a rude bell and then dipping it into melted bronze.

SAINT PATRICK BAPTIZING TWO IRISH MAIDENS

Generally the people were willing to listen to the strangers, but nevertheless, the lives of the missionaries were often in danger. The chiefs were always at warfare among themselves, and it was not safe to go from one district to another without an escort. In one place the people thought the long, narrow writing tablets of the preachers were straight swords, and that they had come to make trouble. It was some little time before they could be made to understand that the strangers were their friends. There is a story that at one time the missionaries were in danger from Laoghaire, the chief king. At twilight King Laoghaire went out with his nobles to light the fire of the spring festival. On the Hill of Slane he saw another fire. It was forbidden on pain of death that anyone else should kindle a fire so long as the king's was burning, and Laoghaire sent men to learn who these daring strangers were and to bring them before him. It is thought that Patrick's poem, called *The Deer's Cry*, was written at this time. Part of it is as follows:—

> At Tara to-day in this fateful hour,
> I place all heaven with its power,
> And the sun with its brightness,
> And the snow with its whiteness,
> And fire with all the strength it hath,
> And lightning with its rapid wrath,
> And the winds with their swiftness along their path,
> And the sea with its deepness,
> And the rocks with their steepness,
> And the earth with its starkness:

> All these I place,
> By God's almighty help and grace,
> Between myself and the Powers of Darkness.

The thought of the poem is that everything that God has made will help to guard the man who puts trust in His protection. The missionaries told the king that their fire was not to celebrate the coming of spring, but Easter and the resurrection of Christ. He listened closely, and finally gave them permission to preach to his people.

The grateful Irish loved Saint Patrick and were eager to make him gifts, but he would never accept them. There is a pretty story that the little son of an Irishman whom he had baptized loved the good preacher so dearly that when the tired man had fallen asleep, the child would creep up softly and lay sweet-scented flowers upon his breast. The boy afterward became a bishop and succeeded his beloved master.

For many years, Saint Patrick preached and taught and built churches and schoolhouses and monasteries. These monasteries, and others that were founded not long afterward, became the most famous schools of the age. Thousands of pupils came to them from the neighbouring countries; and from these seats of learning and piety earnest teachers and missionaries went forth, not only to Britain, but to every corner of Europe. This is the work that was begun by one fearless, faithful, unselfish man.

CHAPTER XIII

THE LEGEND OF KING ARTHUR

THE old legends say that the Teutons who invaded Britain were opposed most valiantly by Arthur, a British king. Tales of his valiant deeds were told over and over again, and new ones were often added. By and by they were put into book form by one Thomas Malory, and it is from this that Tennyson took the stories that he made into the splendid verse of his *Idylls of the King*.

These stories say that after the death of Arthur's father, King Uther, the little boy was brought up by one Sir Ector and was called his son. When Arthur had grown old enough to be a squire, the throne of Britain became vacant. In the church-yard there was seen a great stone, wherein was an anvil. In the anvil was a sword, and about it was written in letters of gold, "Whoso pulleth this sword from this stone and anvil is rightwise king born of all England." Many tried to lift the sword, but Arthur was the only one who succeeded. Therefore he was made king, and he swore that he would rule justly and truly all the days of his life.

Arthur and the enchanter Merlin rode one day by a broad lake, and afar out in the midst of the lake an arm clad in white samite—a rich cloth like satin—rose from out the water and held up a fair sword. Then came the Lady of the Lake moving upon the water. "Enter into yonder barge," she said, "and row to the sword and take it and the scabbard." So it was that King Arthur found his magic sword Excalibur, which so often helped him to overcome his enemies in battle.

KING ARTHUR
OBTAINS THE SWORD
EXCALIBUR

The barons wished the king to take a wife, and Merlin asked, "Is there any fair lady that you love better than another?" "Yes," the king replied, "I love Guinevere. She is the gentlest and fairest lady that I know living." The father of Guinevere consented joyfully to the marriage, and as her dowry he sent the famous Round Table which King Uther had given him long before, with one hundred knights, brave and true. Then Arthur rejoiced. He welcomed Guinevere and he sought out twenty-eight knights of his own to sit at the Round Table, and it was found that by some

THE COURT OF KING ARTHUR
Evelyn Paul

magic the name of each knight had been written upon his seat, or siege, in letters of gold; but on one seat, called the Siege Perilous, there was none.

The bravest of these knights was Lancelot, but they were all strong and valiant. They jousted, they avenged maidens in distress, and they punished all wrongdoing that came to their ears. They were brave and true, but no one of them had dared to place himself in the Siege Perilous. At last there came to Arthur's court a fair and pure youth named Galahad, and when the silken cloth was lifted from the Siege Perilous, behold, upon it was written, "This is the seat of Galahad."

One evening, when every knight sat in his place, a cracking was heard and the sound of thunder, and a sunbeam seven times brighter than day was seen, and in the sunbeam was the Holy Grail, the cup from which the Blessed Christ drank at the Last Supper. But it was veiled with white samite, so that none might see it. Thereupon most of the knights took vows that they would search the world over till the glorious vision of the Grail should come to them. It was a long and almost hopeless search. Even the pure Sir Galahad made many journeys in vain, but at last he had a vision of the Holy Cup. Then a multitude of angels bore his soul to heaven, and never again has the Grail been seen upon the earth.

At length, King Arthur was sorely wounded in battle, and he knew that the time had come for him to die. "Cast my sword Excalibur into the water of the lake," he bade Sir Bedivere, his companion, "and come again and tell me what you have seen." And when Sir Bedivere had thrown the sword, there rose from the water an arm clad with white samite. The hand took the sword and both sword and arm vanished beneath the waters. Then came close to the shore a barge, and in it was King Arthur's sister with two other queens and many fair ladies in waiting. The king was laid softly into the barge, and Sir Bedivere went away into the forest to weep.

THE THREE QUEENS MOURNING OVER KING ARTHUR

In the morning, he came upon a chapel wherein was a tomb by which a hermit was praying. The hermit told Sir Bedivere that the man who was buried in the tomb had been brought there by some ladies at midnight. Then the faithful knight knew that it was the tomb of his king, and by it he abode all the days of his life, fasting and praying for the soul of his lord, King Arthur.

CHAPTER XIV

KING ALFRED THE GREAT

I T was about 449 when the Teutons landed on the island of Thanet. More and more of them came, until finally not the Britons, but the Teutons, ruled England. Each company tried to make their settlement a little kingdom by itself. Sometimes a little group of these kingdoms were allies for a

while, then they were enemies. Gradually the West Saxons became more powerful than the others, and at length their king, Egbert, induced seven of these kingdoms to make a sort of union.

HILTS OF DANISH
IRON SWORDS

It would have been far better if this union could have been strong and lasting, for all England was now in dreadful peril. The reason was that still more tribes were pushing on to the westward. These tribes were Teutons who lived in Norway, Sweden, and Denmark; but the English called them all Danes. The Danes thought it a disgrace to live quietly on the land, and they dashed off in the fiercest tempests and over the stormiest seas in search of treasure.

THE STATUE OF KING ALFRED AT WINCHESTER
Hamo Thorneycroft, R. A.

They would steal up to a church or a convent or a village in the mist and darkness. Then with wild shouts to Odin and Thor they would kill, burn, and plunder. They destroyed bridges, they set fire to the growing crops, they tossed little babies to and fro on the points of their spears, they tortured the helpless dogs and horses. Then they set off for their home-land to display the treasures they had won. Their code of honour was that a Dane who fled from fewer than five disgraced himself. The warriors had no fear of death, for they believed that the Valkyries would come and carry those slain in battle to the delights of Valhalla.

These were the enemies whom the grandson of Egbert, the Saxon king Alfred, a young man of twenty-three, had to meet. At the death of his brother he had become king, but just at that time the Danes were coming in throngs and there were no rejoicings in honour of the new sovereign. There was no feasting, there was not even a meeting of the councillors of the kingdom to declare that they accepted him as their ruler. The Danes landed first on one shore, then on another. Alfred built warships and won a battle on the sea. Then he was surprised by the Danes and most of his people were subdued. Their king, however, had no thought of yielding. He and some of his faithful followers withdrew to Athelney, an island in the swampy forest of Somer-set, where they made themselves a fort. A few people lived in this wilderness who tended the swine of their lord. Their homes were tiny huts of brush-wood plastered with mud. Two legends of his stay at

Athelney have been handed down to us. One is that he once took refuge in one of these tiny huts, much to the wrath of the housewife, for her husband had not told her who was his guest. The story says that she bade the visitor sit by the fire and turn her cakes when they were done on one side. The anxious king forgot all about them, and the angry housewife scolded. According to an old ballad, she cried,—

> "There, don't you see the cakes are burnt?
> Then wherefore turn them not?
> You're quick enough to eat them
> When they are good and hot."

ALFRED THE GREAT LETTING THE CAKES BURN

The second legend is that in order to find out the number of the Danes he put on the dress of a harper and went to the Danish camp. There he sang old ballads, perhaps even part of *Beowulf*. The Danes were delighted, and never guessed that they were applauding the king of the English. Alfred went back to his friends with a good knowledge of the Danish camp and a heart full of courage. When the spring came, he surprised his enemies and forced them to promise to be baptized as Christians. He was not strong enough to drive them from the country, but it was agreed that they should remain in their settlements in the eastern and northern parts of England, while Alfred should rule the southern and western parts. Then Alfred set to work to do what he could for his kingdom.

AN EARLY ENGLISH CHURCH
(Church of St. Lawrence, Wiltshire, built probably
in the 7th century)

The king of England was in a hard position. Much of the country had been ravaged again and again. Churches, libraries, and convents had been destroyed. Alfred built a line of forts around the south-eastern coast, for he knew that other Danes would be likely to come. He built at least one hundred warships. He made a code of laws for his people. He appointed judges, who were punished if they were not just. One judge was hanged because he condemned a man unlawfully. Alfred built churches and convents. He brought learned men to his kingdom, following the example of Charlemagne in earlier times. He established schools, and he commanded that every freeborn boy in the kingdom should learn to read English, and that if he showed ability, he should go on and learn to read Latin. Now arose a difficulty. In those times books were written in Latin as a matter of course, and there were very few in English. So the busy king set to work to translate books for his people. One of them was a sort of history and geography combined. In this is the story which Longfellow has put into his poem, *The Discoverer of the North Cape*—the story of

> Othere the old sea-captain
> Who dwelt in Helgoland.

Alfred had received a barren land, overrun by enemies. He left it a peaceful, prosperous kingdom with schools, churches, just laws, vessels, and fortifications. It is no wonder that he is called Alfred the Great.

CHAPTER XV

RURIK THE NORSEMAN

T HE people who lived in the central part of Russia in the ninth century did not all belong to any one nation. Many tribes had come from Asia and passed through the land, and some members of the tribes went no farther. These people were tall and strong. They could climb cliffs which one would think only goats could scale; and they could swim across the swiftest rivers. They taught their children that every injury must be avenged, and that it was a disgrace to forgive a wrong.

They had no idea of what it meant to be afraid, and when they went to battle, it was the same to them whether they were fighting with some tribe as wild as themselves or with the well-trained Roman soldiers, and they had but one fashion of attack; when the enemy drew near, the whole body flung themselves furiously upon their foes. If they had once taken any plunder, they would die rather than give it up, no matter how useless it might be to them.

There are two good things to say about these people. The first is that they were kind to one another. The second is that they were most hospitable. They had a custom of putting some food in sight when they left their huts, so that no chance wayfarer need go away hungry. Indeed, their hospitality went so far that if a stranger came to them and they had no food for him, it was regarded as entirely proper to steal whatever was needed.

SCENE IN NORTH RUSSIA
(Showing the marshes)

They believed in a great god, whom they called the Thunder-maker, and in a vast number of less powerful gods. They never thought of their deities as kind and gentle, but always as fierce and savage, and they carved most hideous images, into which they believed the spirits of the gods would enter that they might be worshipped.

After a while the wisest and bravest among them became chiefs. Still, they were a rude, savage folk, and some tribes were more like beasts than human beings.

In northern Russia, around the Baltic Sea, lived people who were more fierce than these in Central Russia. They were always ready to leap into their boats and go as fast as wind and oars would carry them wherever they thought they could find

NORSE SHIPS

plunder. These were the people whom the English called Danes. They were also called Northmen or Norsemen, because they came from the north, and Vikings, which meant pirates. Some of them entered the service of the emperors at Constantinople. They were most loyal bodyguards and they could be trusted freely with the keys of both palace and treasury. In battle they were valuable friends, but sometimes the officers must have been a little puzzled to know how to manage them. Once the odds were so much against them that the Greek commander, whose allies they were, sent a herald to them to ask, "Will you fight, or will you retreat?" "We will fight," the Northmen shouted; and one of them was so enraged at the suggestion of retreat that he gave the herald's horse such a blow with his fist as to strike it dead.

The Northmen usually went to Constantinople by launching their boats in the headwaters of the Dnieper River and floating down to the Black Sea. They had seen a good deal of the world, and they were bright and keen. They succeeded in making the people of Central Russia pay them tribute. According to the old story, there came a time when the people determined not to pay it any longer. They united and drove the Northmen away. But they did not stay united. They quarrelled among themselves, for each man did whatever he chose and no one cared for the rights of his neighbour. It is said that one among them, who was wiser than the rest saw that they needed some ruler to govern them. He knew how much more civilized the Northmen were, and he persuaded several of the tribes about him to send envoys to the Russ, a tribe of Northmen, to say, "Our country is large and rich, but we have no order. Do you come and rule over us." A

RURIK

93

Northman named Rurik and his two brothers said, "We will come"; and the three set out with their followers, all well armed, as were those who had come as envoys. Rurik built his stronghold at Novgorod; one brother went farther south, and the other farther north-east. After a year or two, the younger brothers died and Rurik was left to rule alone. He chose men whom he could trust, and gave them land. In return, they built fortresses and helped him to keep peace in the land, to govern the unruly tribes, and to teach them to obey. As soon as he had them well in hand, he conquered neighbouring tribes; and so his little kingdom grew rapidly, until it became a large kingdom, which took the name of Russia from the Russ tribe. Rurik himself was now called grand-prince or *veliki knias.*

After Rurik had reigned for seventeen years, he died, leaving his throne to his little son. So it was that the first ruler of Russia was a bold and daring warrior, and the second a boy only four years old.

CHAPTER XVI

ROLLO THE VIKING

THE story is told that while Charlemagne was sitting one day at dinner, a fleet of long, narrow boats came swiftly toward the land. "Those must have come from Brittany," some one declared; and another said, "No, they are surely Jewish merchantmen." But Charlemagne had noted the vessels, that they had only one sail, that bow and stern were shaped alike and were gilded and carved to represent the head or tail of a dragon, and that a row of shields was ranged along the gunwale. "Those bring nothing to sell," he said. "They are most cruel foes, they are Northmen." Then there was a hurrying and scurrying to put on armour, snatch up swords and spears, and hasten to the shore to drive away the pirates. But the Northmen had heard of the prowess of Charlemagne, and as soon as they knew he was there they rowed away as fast as their boats could be made to carry them. The Franks had much to say about these enemies, but Charlemagne stood silent, gazing at the sea. At length he turned toward his friends. His eyes were full of tears, and he said, "I am not afraid that the

Northmen will harm me, but I weep to see that they have ventured so near our shore, and to think of the evils that they will bring upon my children and their people."

Charlemagne was right, for it was not many years after his death before one hundred and twenty pirate vessels were rowed swiftly up the River Seine, and a horde of Northmen, or Vikings, poured into the little city of Paris, ready to kill, burn, and steal, as usual. But suddenly a heavy fog hid them from one another. There was some enchantment about it, they thought, and they made their way back to their ships as best they might. They came again and again, however. Sometimes they were met with arms, some times with tribute. Still they came. "Did not we promise you twelve thousand pounds of silver if you would leave us in peace?" demanded the Franks in despair. "The king promised it," replied the Northmen insolently, "and we left him in peace. He is dead now, and what we do will not disturb him."

The following year the famous leader Rollo led the Vikings in an attack upon Paris. They hammered at the walls of the city with battering-rams. With great slings they hurled stones and leaden balls. They dug a mine under one of the walls, leaving wooden props. Then they set fire to these and scrambled out of the narrow passage as fast as they could. The beams burned and the earth fell in, but the walls did not crumble as the Vikings had hoped. Then they built a fire close to the wooden walls, but a sudden rain put it out. There were thirty or forty thousand of the Vikings, and only two hundred of the Franks in the besieged city; but the Franks had wise leaders, and all this time they were boiling oil and pitch and pouring them down upon the besiegers. The blazing Northmen leaped into the river to extinguish the flames, but they never thought of giving up. They collected food and encamped near the city. Month after month the siege went on, and still the king did not come to help his brave people.

ROUTES OF THE VIKING EXPEDITIONS

At last the valiant Eudes, or Odo, one of the chief leaders of the Parisians, determined to go in search of aid, and one stormy night he managed to slip through the gate of the city and the lines of the Northmen, and gallop off to the king. Soon the king came with his army—and went into camp! After he had dawdled a month away, news came that more Vikings were at hand. The king was so frightened that he offered the Northmen seven hundred pounds of silver if they would depart, and told them they might go farther up the river and plunder Burgundy as much as they chose. The brave defenders of Paris were indignant. They rushed out of the city and struck one fierce blow at their departing foes. The following year the cowardly king was deposed, and at his death they chose the valiant Eudes for their ruler.

The Northmen were bright, shrewd people; and, wild as they were, they could not help seeing that the Frankish way of living was better than theirs, and that the worship of the Christian God was better than that of Odin and Thor. Rollo led them again to France some years later, and this time the Vikings ranged themselves on one side of a little river, and the king with his Franks stood on the other side, to talk about peace. Rollo was willing to give up his pirate life, be baptized, and live in the Frankish country if the king would give him land. "I will give you Flanders," said the king; but Rollo replied, "No, that is too swampy." "Then you may have the parts of Neustria[1] nearest to the shore." "No," declared

[1] The western kingdom of the Franks.

Rollo, "that is nothing but forest land." At length it was agreed that he and his followers should have the land which afterward took its name from them and to this day is called Normandy. They were to hold it by what is known as a feudal tenure, that is, it was to be theirs so long as they were faithful to the king and gave him loyal military service.

RUINS OF AN ANCIENT CASTLE IN NORMANDY
(At Dieppe, France. This view shows typical Normandy scenery)

There is a story that the bishops told Rollo he must kiss the king's foot in token of his having received this great gift and having become the king's vassal. The haughty Northman had no idea of doing any such thing; but when the bishops insisted, he motioned to one of his warriors to do it for him. The warrior was as proud as his lord. The old account says that he would not kneel, but lifted the royal foot so high that the king fell backward. The Franks were angry, but the Northmen roared with laughter.

The Northmen, or Normans, as they were afterwards called, went into their new domain. Rollo ruled them strictly, for he was as anxious to be a successful ruler as he had been to be a successful pirate. The same story is told of him that is related of Alfred the Great and several other kings, that one might leave a golden bracelet hanging on a tree in perfect safety anywhere in his possessions. Whether that is true or not, it is true that any robber who fell into the hands of Rollo was promptly hanged. It is also true that it was exceedingly difficult for a criminal to escape, because Rollo made the whole land responsible for him. Whenever anyone committed a trespass, the first man who found it out must cry "Haro!" and the cry must go through the whole kingdom until the man was captured.

So it was that the Vikings who had come to France to plunder, gave up their wild, savage life and became permanent dwellers in that country.

CHAPTER XVII

WILLIAM THE CONQUEROR

THE Danes not only invaded France and set-tled in that land, but they won so much power in England that a little more than a century after the death of Alfred the Great, one of them drove away the weak king Ethelred and took possession of the English throne. The son of this Dane was the famous Canute. Canute was not only kind and just to his English subjects, but he seemed to love them and to wish to do his best for them. During his absence from England on one occasion, he left the government in the hands, not of a Dane, but of an Englishman. Canute was a very sensible man, and he disliked flattery more than kings are usually supposed to do. Once when his foolish courtiers assured him that even the sea would obey him, he bade them place his chair on the beach. Then he gravely ordered the ocean to retreat and not wet even the border of his robe. The courtiers stood about him in some alarm, for they were afraid of being punished for their untruthfulness. Soon the waves splashed the king, and then he turned to the flatterers and said gently, "He who is King of Kings,

CANUTE ORDERS THE OCEAN TO RETREAT

and Lord of Lords, He is the one whom the earth and the sea and the heavens obey."

Ethelred had fled to Normandy, and there his son Edward afterward known as the Confessor, grew up. His mother was a Norman, and his own ways of thinking were French rather than English. After Canute's two sons had died, the English sent for Edward to come and rule over them. The young Duke William of Normandy, a bold, ambitious man, was his friend and kinsman, and Edward promised to bequeath to him the English throne. After Edward had been in England a while, however, he learned that he could not give away the throne as if it were a bag of gold, but that the English people had something to say about who should rule them. When Edward died, therefore, they asked a brave English-man named Harold to become their king.

Duke William of Normandy was indignant. He was a descendant of Rollo and was as energetic as the Viking himself. He set out with a great force of men and ships to seize the kingdom that he believed was justly his own. He sailed straight for the English coast, and not a ship came out to fight him. He landed at Pevensey near Hastings, and not a man cast a spear at him. He began to pillage the country, and no one opposed him. There were good reasons why the English were so quiet. One was that their fleet was made up of fishing vessels, which now scattered here and there, for according to cus-tom their owners were allowed at stated times to take them away in order to attend to their fishing. Secondly, the army was made up chiefly of farmers, and they had been permitted to go home to attend to their harvesting. Harold, meanwhile, was in the north with a few followers, repelling an invasion of the Danes, led by his brother Tostig and Harold Hardrada. These he conquered at Stamford Bridge;

THE WOUNDING OF HAROLD AT THE BATTLE OF HASTINGS

then making a rapid march to the south he brought together what troops he could, and with no chance to train them, he fought a fierce battle with the Normans, and was defeated. It is possible that the invaders might not have won the day if they had not used a favourite trick of their pirate ancestors of pretending to run away. The English forgot their orders to keep in their places and dashed forward in pursuit. Then, when they were unprotected and scattered, the Normans suddenly turned upon them and overcame them, and Harold was slain. This was the famous battle of Hastings, or Senlac, one of the most important battles in all English history, because it decided that England should be ruled by the Normans. In France there are some very interesting pictures of this invasion embroidered upon a strip of linen seventy yards long called the Bayeux Tapestry.

BATTLE OF HASTINGS
(From the Bayeux Tapestry)

These pictures look as if a little child had drawn them, but there is a good deal of life in them, and they do tell the story. It is possible that they were worked by William's wife, Matilda, and her ladies in waiting.

105

WILLIAM ENTERING LONDON

After the battle of Senlac, William marched to London. No one dared to oppose him, and the chief men of the nation went to his camp and asked him to become their ruler. So on Christmas Day, 1066, William the Conqueror, as he is known in history, was crowned king in Westminster Abbey by the Archbishop of York.

The English watched anxiously to see how their new sovereign would treat them. Those who wished to keep their land had to go to him and swear to be faithful. The land of those who would not take the oath and of those who had fought at Hastings came into his hands, and he gave it to his Norman followers. He also gave the highest offices in church and state to Normans. That was natural; but it was hard for the English to bear, especially as the Normans looked upon them as rude, ignorant folk, much their inferiors. The English rose against William again and again. Four years after the battle of Hastings, a valiant leader named Hereward, with a large number of men, encamped on the Isle of Ely[1] and resisted him for more than a year. William built a causeway through the marsh that surrounded the island, but for a long time his efforts to break up the Camp of Refuge, as it was called, were unsuccessful. Finally, through treachery some believe, the English were overcome. Hereward escaped, but this was the last rising of the English against their conqueror.[2]

[1] A marshy plain in Cambridgeshire, north of the River Ouse.
[2] *The Story of Hereward*, by Douglas C. Stedman, B.A.

HEREWARD WATCHES THE BUILDING OF THE CAUSEWAY

William was severe, and those who broke his laws rarely escaped punishment, but even the English admitted that he was just. On one occasion he threw one of his own brothers into prison for wronging his English subjects. Three of his acts, however, they never forgave. One was his driving away the tenants from many thousand acres of land near his palace in Winchester. He may have done this to prevent any sudden attack upon him; but the people believed it was in order to provide him with a convenient hunting ground, the New Forest, as it was called; and they were angry. Again, they were indignant because he ordered that a curfew, or *cover fire*, bell should be rung every evening, and that at its sound all fires should be covered and all lights put out. William may have felt that this was necessary to prevent people from coming together at night to plot against him. Moreover, it was an old French custom to prevent the burning of houses; but the English objected stoutly to being told when they were to go to bed. On the whole, however, nothing else made them quite so angry as William's Dooms-day Book (so called because

THE TOWER OF
LONDON
(Showing in the centre the
White Tower built by
William the Conqueror)

its records were supposed to be final). In order to assess the taxes fairly, he sent men throughout the kingdom to find out just how much property each person owned. The men went into every house, barnyard, and sheepfold, and wrote in their accounts not only who held the land, but even how many animals there were. Then the English were enraged. They were afraid their taxes would be made larger; but, worse than that, they felt that it was a great inso-lence for strange men to come into their homes and write down the value of their property. They had to yield, however, to this and whatever else William thought best to do.

Altogether, the English people were not very happy, but to have such a king was really what they needed. They were a little slow and grave, while William was quick and liked a jest. They were good followers and steady fighters; while William was a bold leader and could change his plans on the battle-field in a moment if those that he had made failed.

William still ruled Normandy, and he had to go back and forth between the two countries. Normandy was a fief of France, that is, it was held by feudal tenure, but it was a most independent duchy, and was not at all afraid to resist the French king. In one of their struggles the city of Mantes was burned. When riding over the ruins, William was thrown from his horse, and afterward died of his injuries. The English royal family is descended from William the Conqueror and Matilda his wife, and Matilda was descended from Alfred the Great; therefore the present king of England represents both Alfred the Great and William the Conqueror.

CHAPTER XVIII

LEIF ERICSSON, THE DISCOVERER

THERE was once a Northman called Eric the Red. For some reason he was exiled to Iceland; but in a little while he was in trouble there also. He had lent his seatposts, or wooden posts carved into images of the gods, which stood by the high seats at the feasts, and the man who held them refused to return them. A quarrel had arisen, and in the course of it Eric had slain the man. For this reason, he was now exiled from Iceland for three years. He knew there was a country lying to the westward, for a sailor caught in a storm had been thrown upon its shores, and he determined to seek it. He found the land and spent two or three years exploring it; then he returned to Iceland. He meant, however, to found a colony in the new country, and therefore he called it Greenland. "People will not like to move there if it has not a good name," declared this wise colonizer. Probably he had obtained some new seatposts by this time; for the custom was to throw them overboard when land was near and to settle wherever they floated ashore.

A few years after Eric founded his colony in Greenland, his son Leif or Leif Ericsson, spent a winter in Norway. There he became a Christian and was baptized. When he was about to return to his home in Greenland, King Olaf of Norway said, "I beg of you to see that the people in Greenland are told of the Christ, for no one is better to attend to this than you."

NORSEMEN LANDING IN ICELAND
Oscar Wergeland

So it came about that when Leif returned to Greenland, he carried with him a priest and several other religious teachers. A little later, he saved a ship's crew from drowning, and because of this people called him Leif the Lucky; but his father said rather grimly that Leif might have done a good thing in saving the men, but he had done a bad thing in bringing a priest to Greenland. After a while, however, Eric himself became a Christian, and so did his wife, and most of the people followed their example.

Now among those who came to Greenland was a man named Biarne. On the voyage he had been blown out of his course close to an unknown land lying to the south of Greenland, and when he finally reached the colony, he told of how he had seen this land. Then Leif and the other young men gathered around him. "What sort of country was it? Were there any people there? What grows in the place? Are there moun-

RUINS OF A CHURCH
IN GREENLAND
(It is supposed to have been one of the churches built by Leif and his followers)

tains or lowlands?" they questioned, and Biarne had to own that he had not gone ashore. "Humph! He was not very eager for knowledge," said the young men rather contemptuously. They talked a great deal about the unknown lands, and finally Leif bought Biarne's ship and made ready to go on a voyage of discovery. "Do you go with us as leader," he urged his father; but Eric replied, "Oh, I am growing too old for a hard voyage at sea." "But no one else of all our kin will be as lucky as you," pleaded Leif, and at length Eric mounted his horse and rode toward the ship. Suddenly the horse slipped and he fell off. That settled the question. "It is fated," he said, "that I should never discover any other land than Greenland," and so Leif and his men were obliged to sail without him.

After a while they came to a shore where lofty mountains rose, covered with snow. This is thought to have been the coast of Labrador. Then they

NORSE BOAT USED
AS A DWELLING

passed a flat and wooded shore, which is believed to have been Nova Scotia. At length they reached a coast that seemed to them most inviting. The shores were of white, shining sand; and beyond them were pleasant woods which seemed to stretch far inland. There were rivers full of salmon and meadows covered with rich grass. Leif and his followers carried their beds to land, set up their tents, and made ready to explore the country. He divided his men into two parties and made them take turns in staying by the camp and going out to explore.

One of the older men on the voyage was a German. One day he came back chattering away in his own language. *"Weintrauben,"* he exclaimed, *"ich habe Weintrauben gefunden!"* The Northmen could not tell what he meant, and at first he was too much pleased and excited to talk Norwegian. At length he told them he had found grapes, such as he used to have when he was a boy, and that was what had pleased him so much. It was because of this discovery that Leif named the country Vinland, or the land of vines. This is thought to have been Rhode Island and the southern part of Massachusetts.

Then the men set to work to gather grapes and hew wood. Toward spring they took their cargo of wood and dried grapes and sailed back to Greenland. This is the story that the Icelandic sagas, or hero stories, tell. The voyage took place in the year 1000, and if we may trust the old saga, Leif Ericsson was the first white man to set foot on the continent of America.

There is a little more of the saga story that ought to be told. After Leif went back to Greenland, a wealthy merchant named Thorfinn Karlsefne went to visit him. On this visit Thorfinn met Gudrid, one of the shipwrecked people whom Leif had rescued so long ago, and married her. She persuaded her husband to go to Vinland to found a colony. The first autumn in the new home their little son, Snorre was born, at

NORSE RUINS IN GREENLAND
(These curious circular piles of stone are usually found in Greenland near the ruins of old Norse churches)

Straumfjord, which is thought to have been what is now Buzzard's Bay. Snorre was the first white child born in Massachusetts. When he was three years old, the colony was given up, and the baby explorer with his parents returned to Greenland. It was a rough voyage, but the little American boy lived through it and became the ancestor of a long line of wise and excellent men.

The sagas tell of many later voyages to America; but at length a terrible plague came upon the northern lands. In Norway six-sevenths of the people died, and Vinland was forgotten.

CHAPTER XIX

HENRY THE FOWLER

ABOUT one hundred years after the death of Charlemagne, one of his descendants, a little boy only six years old, succeeded to a part of his kingdom. Although the child had guardians, they did not seem to be able to defend the crown. There was trouble from without the kingdom and more trouble from within. The trouble from without was because the Hungarians, or Magyars, were making fierce and bloody invasions of the country. The trouble from within came from the five dukes, each of whom was afraid that the others would become more powerful than he. The child-king died when he was only eighteen, and then there was quarrelling indeed, for every duke wanted to be sovereign. At length Conrad, Duke of Franconia, was set upon the throne; but that did not quiet matters, for some of the dukes had not agreed to his election.

Conrad was a gentle, thoughtful man. He defended his people as well as he could, but perhaps the best thing he did for them was to give them a piece of good advice when he was dying. He had sent for the nobles to come to him, and when they stood around his bed, he talked to them as if they were his children and begged them to live peaceably together. "I do now command you," he said, "to choose Henry, Duke of Saxony, for your king. He is a man of energy in battle, and yet he is a strong friend of peace. I can find no one else so well fitted to rule the kingdom, and therefore I send to him the crown and the sceptre and bid him shield and protect the realm."

The nobles were amazed, for this Henry of Saxony had opposed most strongly of them all the election of Conrad; but the more they thought of their king's advice, the more they saw that it was good; and after Conrad was dead they carried the crown and the sceptre to Henry's castle. He was not there. "Where is he?" the nobles demanded, and the attendants replied, "He is in the forest hunting with his falcons."

Then the nobles and their followers set out into the forest to search for a king. It was several days before they found him; and when they did discover him, he was standing in his hunting suit, and on his wrist was a falcon waiting patiently until its master should give it the signal to fly after a wild duck or whatever other bird he was pursuing. The falcon and the Duke were both surprised when the company of nobles and their attendants appeared, and Henry was still more amazed when they showed him the crown and the sceptre and told him that they had followed the will of Conrad and had chosen him for their king. This is the way that Duke Henry of Saxony became King Henry I. of Germany and won his nickname of "the Fowler."

A FAMOUS CASTLE IN GERMANY

The Magyars came upon the land in swarms. Henry met them bravely; but in every battle the invaders had one great advantage—they fought on horseback, while the Germans were skilled only in fighting on foot. Something happened very soon, however, that changed the whole face of matters; Henry captured a Magyar chief, said to have been the king's son. The Magyars were ready to do almost anything to secure his release; and at length Henry said to them, "If you will leave my country and promise to make no attacks upon it for nine years, I will give back your chief and pay you five thousand pieces of gold every year." The Magyars were glad to accept this offer, and soon they were rejoicing over the return of their chief.

Henry, however, was not spending time in rejoicing. He had much business to attend to in the nine years, and he set about it at once. First, he brought his people together in cities which could be fortified, instead of allowing them to live in scattered villages. Next, he trained his men to fight on horseback. To test their ability, he tried his new cavalry in battles with the Danes and some tribes around him. Then he waited.

The Magyars were in no haste to give up the tribute of gold, and when the tenth year had come, they demanded that the king should send it as usual. But now he was ready to fight them, and he refused. They started out with a great army to make this defiant ruler yield; but to their surprise he drove them out of his kingdom. They never succeeded in entering the northern duchies again, and it was many years before they were seen in any part of Germany.

The wisdom and courage of Henry the Fowler brought peace to his country; and when he died, he left to his son Otho a quiet and prosperous kingdom. Otho was quite as energetic as his father. He took the title of Emperor of the Romans, as if his rule were a continuation of the ancient Roman Empire, and for nine hundred years after him every German king claimed the same title.

CHAPTER XX

HUGH CAPET

I T has already been said that Charlemagne was a German. He, of course, spoke German, but even in his day the people in the western part of his kingdom, in what is now the land of France, used a language that was beginning to approach somewhat to what is now known as French. This change had begun long before, in the days when the country fell into the hands of the Romans, who introduced their own language, the Latin.

AN ANCIENT CASTLE AT CLISSON, FRANCE
(The town of Clisson was pillaged by the Normans in the ninth century)

Now if a new language were introduced into any country to-day, few people would speak it correctly, and it was so in France. The people mixed the new tongue with their own. For instance, when a Roman wished to say *of* or *to* he usually added a letter or two to the noun following. The people of France used the prepositions *de* or *à*, and did not trouble themselves to change the noun. Other words or expressions were made simpler or altered in much the same way, and before the end of the tenth century, the people of France were speaking a language that was composed of a little Celtic, a little German, and a great deal of Latin; but the Latin had become quite different from that used in Rome. This mixture was rapidly turning into French as it is spoken to-day.

The French people, then, differed in language from the Germans, and many of the nobles were

A CELEBRATED FEUDAL CASTLE IN TOURAINE, FRANCE (The original structure was built in Hugh Capet's time by one of the great nobles. The present castle dates from 1460)

feeling more and more strongly that they did not wish to be ruled by a German, but by one of themselves, who would talk French and feel and think like a Frenchman, one who would be satisfied with ruling France and would not be ever thinking of forming an empire and becoming emperor.

In 987, there was an excellent opportunity to put a new family upon the throne, for the last of Charlemagne's direct descendants, Louis the Child, had just died. The great barons met together to choose a ruler. They decided upon Duke Hugh Capet, and he became king. He had little more power, however, than some of his counts and dukes; and it may be that he sometimes wished he was still a duke, for some of the nobles refused to accept him as their ruler. There is a story that one of his vassals, that is, one who held land from him by feudal tenure, overran the district of Touraine, and forthwith began to call himself Count of Tours and Poitiers. "Who made you count?" demanded Hugh; and the independent vassal retorted, "Who made you king?" Indeed, if the brave men of Normandy had not stood by him, Hugh would have had a hard struggle to keep his throne. He meant not only to keep it, but to hand it down in his family, and only a few months after his election he asked his nobles to elect his son Robert king also. Then, while he lived, he reasoned shrewdly, Robert would help him govern the kingdom, and at his death there would be no question as to who should rule, and no division of the kingdom. At first the nobles hesitated a little. "We cannot elect two kings in one year," they gave as an excuse; but at length they yielded, and Robert was crowned.

This was the beginning of the rule of the powerful Capetian family which was to hold the throne of France for more than three centuries. Gaul, or France, had been ruled for many years by Romans and by Germans, but Hugh Capet was a Frenchman, ruling French people, the first king of France.

CHAPTER XXI

THE CID

A LITTLE while before Charles Martel fought the battle of Tours and drove the Mohammedans or Moors out of Gaul, they came into Spain, and before long the southern part of that country was in their hands. They became very prosperous, and founded splendid cities, of which the most famous were Granada and Valencia. The earlier comers, the Goths, held the northern part of Spain; and there were continual wars between the two peoples. The Goths, now called Spaniards, also fought among themselves; and in their quarrels they were glad of any one's help, no matter whether he was Christian or Mohammedan. Of all these warriors, Rodrigo Diaz,

THE ALHAMBRA, AT GRANADA, SPAIN, SHOWING COURT OF THE LIONS
(This palace of the Moorish kings was built in the thirteenth and fourteenth centuries. The city of Granada was founded in the eighth century)

or the Cid, was the greatest. The *Poem of the Cid* was afterward written about his exploits, besides a countless number of ballads. The following are some of the stories that were told about him:—

Long before he was made a knight, two of the Spanish kings had a quarrel about a certain city that lay on the line between their two kingdoms. Each wanted it, and the dispute would have come to war if one of them had not suggested that each should choose a warrior, and that single combat should settle the question. One king chose a famous knight, but the other chose the young Rodrigo. "I will gladly fight for you," he said to his king, "but I have vowed to make a pilgrimage, and I must do that first."

A FAMOUS CASTLE AT VALENCIA, SPAIN

So on the pilgrimage he went. On the way he saw a leper who begged for help. Rodrigo helped him out of the bog in which he was fast sinking, set him in front of him on his own horse, and carried him to an inn. There he and the leper used the same trencher, or wooden plate, and they slept in the same bed. In the night Rodrigo awoke with the feeling that some one had breathed upon him so strongly that the breath had passed through his body. The leper was gone, but a vision of St. Lazarus appeared to him and said, "I was the leper whom you helped, and for your kindness God grants that your foes shall never prevail against you." Upon returning from his pilgrimage, Rodrigo vanquished in single contest the knight opposed to him and so gained the city for his king. After this people called him the Campeador, or Champion.

Even before this he had won his title of the Cid, or chief, by overcoming five Mohammedan kings. Instead of putting them to death, however, he had let them go free, and they were so grateful that they agreed to become his vassals, and to send him tribute. But this was not the end of their gratitude. A while later some of the counts of Castile became so envious of the Cid's greatness that they plotted to bring about his death. They made what they thought was a most excellent plan. They wrote to a number of the Moors, saying that in the next battle that should be fought they all intended to desert the Cid; and then, when he was alone, the Moors could easily capture him or slay him. The Moors would have been delighted to do this; but, unluckily for the plotters, some of the letters went to the five kings to whom the Cid had shown mercy. They had not forgotten his kindness; they sent him word of the proposed treachery, and the wicked counts were driven out of the kingdom.

The greatest exploit of the Cid was his capture of the Moorish city of Valencia, the richest city in all Spain. After a siege nine months long, the city yielded; and the people were in terror of what the Cid might do to them for having resisted him so long. But he was a humane warrior. He called the chief men together and told them that they were free to cultivate their lands, and that all he should ask from them was one-tenth of their gains. The ruler of Valencia was a man who had slain their rightful king. While the siege was going on, he had sold food to the starving people at a great price; and after the surrender he offered to the Cid the money that he had made in this way; but the Cid would not accept it, and he put the wicked man to death with many tortures.

The Cid was now a mighty ruler and a very wealthy man. Even the Sultan of far-away Persia sent noble gifts to him and earnestly desired his friendship.

After some years the Cid heard that the king of Morocco was about to come upon him with six and thirty other kings and a mighty force, and he was troubled. But one night St. Peter came to him in a vision. "In thirty days you will leave this world," he said, "but do you atone for your sins, and you shall enter into the light. Be not troubled about the coming of the Moors upon your people, for even though you are dead, you shall win the battle for them."

Then the Cid made himself ready for death. He ordered that, after he was dead, his people should put his body in battle array with helmet and armour, with shield and sword, and fix it firmly upon his horse with arm upraised as if to strike. This they did, and they went forth with the body of the Cid at their head to meet the six and thirty kings. The knights of the Cid came so suddenly and fought so fiercely that the six and thirty kings fled, and galloped their horses even into the sea. "We saw an amazing sight," the Moors afterwards declared, "for there came upon us full 70,000 knights, all as white as snow. And before them rode a knight of great stature, sitting upon a white horse with a bloody cross. In one hand he bore a white banner, and in the other a sword which seemed to be of fire, and he slew many."

Twenty-two of the six and thirty kings were slain. The others went their way and never even turned their heads. Then when the body of the Cid had been lifted down from the horse, his friends robed it in cloth of purple and set it in the ivory chair of the conqueror, with his sword Tizona in its hand. And after ten years it was buried close by the altar of St. Peter in a monastery at Cardena.

One of his followers cared for Banieca, the horse that had been so dear to the Cid. Every day he led it to water and led it back and gave it food with his own hand. When the horse died, he buried it before the gate of the monastery. He set an elm at its head and another at its feet, and he bade that, when he himself should die, he should be buried beside the good horse Banieca whom he had loved so well, and for whom he had cared so tenderly.

THE CID'S LAST BATTLE
O. Knille

CHAPTER XXII

MAGNA CHARTA

LESS than two hundred years after the reign of William the Conqueror one of his descendants, King John, sat upon the throne of England. He was an exceedingly bad ruler. He stole, he told lies, and he put innocent people in prison. If he wanted money, he simply demanded it of any persons who had it, and if they refused to give it, he did not hesitate to torture them till they yielded. Men who had committed crime and deserved to be punished he would set free if they could raise money enough to make him a present. If two men disagreed and brought their difficulty before him for trial, he would decide in favour of the one who had made him the larger gift. Sometimes, for some very small offence, he would demand money of a poor man who had only a horse and cart with which to earn his living; and if the man had no friends to bribe the king, his horse and cart were sold to help fill the royal treasury. King John was even believed to have murdered a nephew, the young Prince Arthur, who had claim to the throne.

John ruled not only England, but also the duchy of Normandy, which had descended to him from William the Conqueror. As Normandy was a fief of France, Philip, King of France, called upon his vassal John to account for the death of the prince. John refused to appear. Then Philip took away nearly all his French possessions. That loss made his income much smaller. Moreover, the cost of carrying on the government had increased. There was, then, some reason for his constant need of money, even though there was so little excuse for his manner of obtaining it.

When the Archbishop of Canterbury died, there was a dispute about who should succeed him. The Pope was appealed to, and he bade the monks of Canterbury name a good, upright man named Stephen Langton to take his place. This choice did not please the king, therefore he seized the monastery and its revenues and banished the monks. For six years John resisted the Pope and refused to allow Langton to become archbishop. Finally he became afraid that he was going to die, and then he yielded most meekly. He even went to Langton to beg for absolution, or the pardon of the church. "When you promise to obey the laws of the land and to treat your people justly, I will absolve you," replied the archbishop.

John was always ready to make a promise, but he never kept it unless it was convenient. He promised what the archbishop asked; but, as might have been expected, he soon broke his word.

ARCHBISHOP LANGTON READING THE LAW
OF THE LAND TO THE BARONS

Now, next to the king, the barons were the most powerful men of the kingdom; but even they did not know what to do. Fortunately, the archbishop knew. He called the barons together, and read them what had been the law of the land since a short time after the death of William the Conqueror. Then the barons understood what their rights were, and they took a solemn oath to defend them. "But we will wait for one year," they said. "The king may do better." They waited a year; then they waited till Christmas. The king had not improved, and the barons went to him and asked him to repeat the promises that he had made to the archbishop. John was insolent at first, but when he saw that the barons were in earnest, he became very meek, and said that what they asked was important, to be sure, but also difficult, and he should need a little time before making the agreement. By Easter he should be able to satisfy them. The barons did not believe him, and so, when Easter came, they brought to the appointed place a large body of armed followers. After a while John sent to ask what it was that the barons insisted upon having. Then bold, dignified Stephen Langton read aloud to him from a parchment such articles as these: "A free man shall not be fined for a small offence, except in proportion to the gravity of the offence." "No free man shall be imprisoned or banished except by the lawful judgment of his equals, or by the law of the land."

John grew more and more angry as these were read; and when the archbishop went on to read other articles declaring that the king must not take bribes, or impose taxes without the consent of his council, or body of advisers, and finally one giving the barons the right to elect twenty-five of their number to keep watch over him and seize his castles if he did not keep his promise, then he went into a furious passion. "I will never grant liberties that would make me a slave," he declared.

Nevertheless, he had to yield. There was a famous green meadow with low hills on one side and the River Thames on the other. Its name of Runny-mede, or *Meadow of Council*, was given it long before William the Conqueror landed in England, because there the Saxons used to hold their councils. To this meadow the barons and their army marched from London. Then out of a strong fortress that rose near at hand, and across the drawbridge that swung over the moat, rode an angry and sulky ruler of England. He promised that his seal should be fixed to the parchment, and then he went back to his palace. He was well-nigh mad with rage; but the barons cared little for this, and they caused many copies of this parchment to be made and sent over the land to be read aloud in the churches.

This parchment was the famous Magna Charta, or Great Charter, sealed in 1215. The barons were then the most powerful men of the kingdom, and they saw to it that as long as he lived the king kept his word. About fifty years later, not only the barons but representatives of the towns were admitted to the council. This was the beginning of the English Parliament; and now, if a king ruled unjustly, he must account, not only to the barons, but to the whole people. From that day to this, no monarch has been able to remain on the throne of England who has not kept the promises that King John was obliged to make that June day at Runnymede.

CHAPTER XXIII

THE LIFE OF THE KNIGHT

WHEN a knight galloped into the courtyard of a castle, his helm and armour glittering, his sword clanking at his side, his plume waving, and his horse prancing and caracoling, it is small wonder if the boys of the place gathered to see him, and if each said to himself, "I wish I were a knight."

The boy who was to be a knight must be of noble birth. His training generally began when he was only seven or eight years old. He was taken away from his mother and his father's castle, for it was the custom for boys to be brought up in the castle of some friend of their father's or perhaps of some one of higher rank than he. A castle was a gloomy stone building, with strong walls and towers, usually placed either high up on a cliff or in a swamp, so that it could not be easily captured. Within it were dungeons and treasure rooms and rooms for the lord and his family. It had also a well and perhaps a garden, and it was protected by a moat and a drawbridge.

The little boy about to begin his training at such a castle was first called a page; and before he could hope to become even a squire there was much for him to learn. Until he was fourteen or fifteen his first business was to wait upon the ladies of the household, to run on their errands, carry messages for them, and ride with them when they went out hunting or hawking. He must always be polite and obedient, for no one could imagine such a thing as a knight who was rude or would not obey the laws of

A CASTLE IN SUSSEX, ENGLAND
(Built in the fourteenth century. The moat is shown in the foreground)

knighthood. He must learn to play chess and draughts, to read, to sing, to dance, to play on the flute and harp, and to say his catechism. He was also taught that he must choose some lady and must serve her truly. There is a story that a lady of the French court once asked a little page who was the mistress of his heart. "I love my mother best and my sister next," he replied. "Yes, but who is your lady-love in chivalry?" she asked, and he finally chose a little ten-year old girl. "That is not the way," declared his teacher. "You must not choose a child, but some lady of noble birth who can advise and help you. Some day you must do daring deeds for her sake, and you must be so humble and faithful to her that she cannot help being kind to you."

Most of the training of the page was given him by the ladies of the household; but he was also taught to ride and leap, to hurl a light spear, and to fight in sham battles with the other pages of the castle. He waited upon his lord and the ladies at the table, and sometimes he accompanied his lord to battle. He did no fighting there, but simply served in any way that a boy could. He was in no danger, for it would have been a disgrace to any knight to wound a page.

Of course all this time the boy was looking forward to the day when he would be promoted and would become a squire. That came to pass when he was about fourteen. Then he not only served at table and brought water for the lord and his guests to wash their hands before and after the meal, but he learned to carve, he brought his lord's special cup of wine at retiring, and waited upon him in every way. In a large castle where there were many squires, one cared for the dining hall, arranged it for singing or made the tables ready for chess. A squire was not permitted to sit at table with a knight, not even if the knight was his own father, but he might join in the amusements. Each in turn was "squire of the body," and the one in office was he whom all the others envied, for when his lord went to battle, this squire was his regular attendant. The young page might carry the helm, but the squire bore the armour and shield, and it was his task—no easy one—to encase his lord in the heavy armour that was then worn. If the knight lost his weapon, the squire must be ready with another. If he took prisoners, they were handed over to the squire to guard; and if the knight was thrown from his horse, the squire must help him to mount again.

Although a squire was rarely made a knight before he was twenty or twenty-one, he had little chance to be idle. He was still expected to keep up his attendance upon the ladies of the castle; but he now learned to use, not the light weapons with which he had practiced as a page, but the battle-axe and sword and lance of the knight. He must become a master of horsemanship and be perfect in leaping and swimming and climbing. He must learn to bear heat and cold and hunger without a word of complaint, and he must accustom himself to wearing the heavy armour of the time and to moving easily in it. There was one exercise in particular which he was expected to practice until he had become perfect. This was called the quintain. A figure of a man arrayed with sword and shield as if for battle was fastened to a post in such a way that it swung about easily. The young squire rode up to the figure full tilt and struck it with his lance. If he hit it on the breast, nothing happened, but if he aimed badly and hit the legs or the arms or was slow in getting away, then the courtyard re-echoed with shouts of laughter, for the figure whirled about and the unskilful squire was struck a heavy blow with a sandbag.

When the time had come for the young man to become a knight, there was much ceremony, and every act had its meaning. He went into a bath and

A SQUIRE BECOMING
A KNIGHT

afterward put on a white garment to indicate purity. A red one was placed over it to show that he would shed his blood for the right. One whole night he spent fully armed, praying and meditating in a church. On the following day he gave his sword to the priest, who laid it upon the altar, blessed it, and returned it. He made solemn vows to defend the church, to be true to the king, and to help every lady who was in distress. Then the knight of highest rank came forward. The young man knelt before him with clasped hands and declared solemnly that his earnest wish was to maintain religion and chivalry. After this, the knights and ladies put on, first, his spurs, then the other pieces of his armour. The chief knight fixed on the sword and struck him upon the neck a slight blow called the accolade, and said aloud, "I dub thee knight in the name of God and the saints." The other knights embraced him, and the priest prayed that he might ever be faithful and loyal. Then the people all went out of the church, and the newly made knight sprang upon his horse and rode about in his gleaming armour, flashing his sword and spurring on his steed to prance and curvet and caracol. After this he dismounted. He made as generous gifts as he could afford to the servants and minstrels of the castle in which he had received his training. The rest of the day was given to feasting and entertainments.

THE VIGIL
J. Pettie, R. A.

Of course this ceremony differed somewhat in different countries, and sometimes a man was made a knight on the battlefield, because he had just performed some deed of valour. If a knight broke his vows, his spurs were cut off, his sword broken over his head, his armour taken from him, and he was laid in a coffin. Then the burial service was read over him as if he were dead.

The great pleasure and amusement of the knights was the tournament, or mock battle, and they would journey long distances to see one or take part in one. The battle took place in what was called the lists, a large oblong space marked off by railings. Close to these were the galleries, or seats for the spectators. It was all made as gorgeous as possible with a vast display of banners and tapestry and coats of mail, and especially by the brilliant robes of the ladies. When the trumpet sounded and the cry was heard, "Come forth, knights, come forth!" the two bodies of knights that were to tilt, one against the other, galloped forward at full speed from opposite ends of the lists with their lances in rest and met with a terrible shock. The ribbons of their lady-loves waved from their helmets. Pieces of wood were fastened to the points of the lances, for the object of the charge was not to kill but to unhorse opponents. There were strict rules for the behaviour of knights during a tournament, and an accurate method of counting their honours. To strike an opponent out of his sad-

A KNIGHT IN ARMOUR

dle counted three, to break a lance on his helm counted ten. The ladies were the judges of all questions, but they usually resigned their power into the hands of an umpire called the Knight of Honour. After the tournament had come to an end, some fair lady who had been chosen Queen of Beauty and Love, presented the prizes.

Knighthood flourished from the eleventh to the fifteenth centuries. Armour grew heavier and heavier till it became almost impossible for a knight to mount his horse without help, and if his horse was slain, he rolled off helplessly and became an easy prey for his foes. About the middle of the fourteenth century, the English won two great battles, at Crécy and at Poitiers, against the French, not by the power of the knights, but by the valour of the foot soldiers with their bows and arrows. Then came the invention of gunpowder, and after that the knight became little more than a useless encumbrance. His time was past, and his armour is now exhibited as a curiosity in museums.

CHAPTER XXIV

COUNTRY LIFE IN THE MIDDLE AGES

T HE people of the Middle Ages would have thought it exceedingly strange for one man to ask another the price of a piece of land, pay for it, and then call it his own. As a general thing, they obtained land in quite a different fashion. The theory was that the king owned the whole country. But he could not cultivate it all, or even defend it with his single sword. Therefore he gave the use of large districts to his chief men. Each man, when he received a share, knelt before the king with uncovered head, laid his hands in those of his sovereign, and vowed to be his man and to serve him faithfully. Then the king kissed his vassal, or liegeman, and gave him a bit of turf and a twig to indicate that he was to hold the land and what grew upon it. Often when land was granted to a man, he was required to make a small payment of money or produce. This was not rent, but merely an acknowledgment that the property was not his, but his lord's. It was sometimes nothing more than a measure of grain, or a fish or two from some river flowing through the land. In 1492, a piece of land in Newcastle-on-Tyne, was granted on condition that a red rose be paid every midsummer day, if it should be called for.

The service that the king wanted for his grants was almost always service in war. When there was need of fighting, he had a right to call out his vassal to fight for him. But every vassal divided his land into portions and gave it to people who were *his* vassals and had vowed to be faithful to *him*. Therefore when the king needed men he called out his vassals, the great nobles. They called out their vassals, and these vassals called

ENGLISH MANOR HOUSE (Built in the latter half of the twelfth century)

out those who were under them; and all had to go forth to do battle. This was the feudal system. It was a sort of endless chain, except that it did finally come to an end in the manor, or village. Exactly how it arose is still a subject of great dispute.

The early manor usually consisted of one house of fair size, perhaps even a castle, and, gathered around it, a number of little cottages. These were thatched with straw and had generally only one room. The large house was the abode of the lord of the manor, and the little houses were the homes of his tenants. Some of these were called "free" tenants, and they generally paid in money for the use of the land and the protection of their lord. The others were called serfs, or villeins, from the word vill, meaning village. They paid some rent in money or in fowls or produce, and they also had to spend a goodly share of their time, sometimes as much as half of it, working on the land which the lord reserved for himself. The lord of a manor always had a list of the tenants, called an "extent," which stated what each one was bound to pay and what work he

OLD COUNTRY HOUSE
(Said to be the oldest house on the Rhine)

must do. For instance, on one manor a man who had a cottage and an acre of land had to pay at the feast of Saint Michael threepence,[1] and at Christmas a cock and a hen worth threepence. Another, who had only a little piece of land, had to bring to his lord one goose, worth twopence, every year. The labour varied greatly in kind and in amount. One man, among other sorts of work, had to provide "a cart and three animals of his own," and carry wood from the forest to the manor house two days every summer. This was worth ninepence, but his lord was to give him three meals worth twopence, halfpenny each. Twice every summer he was to carry half a load of grain; but his meals in this case were not to be so extravagant, for they were to be worth only twopence each.

---

[1] Of course threepence in those days was worth much more than the same small sum to-day.

The arable land of the manor was divided into three or more great fields. One field was planted with wheat or rye, another with oats or peas or barley, and the third field lay fallow for a season. The next year the arrangement was changed about, and thus every field had its rotation of crops and its year of rest. These lands were divided among the tenants in what seems now a strange fashion. They were marked off into strips, usually forty rods long and four rods wide, and instead of a tenant's having a field to himself, he had a certain number of strips. Moreover, these were not together, but were scattered, one or two in a place. Even the lord's land was generally scattered in the same way.

The villeins were not allowed to leave the manor; and if it passed into the hands of another owner, they went with it as the oxen or the houses did. And even if a man wished to run away, where could he go? The whole country was divided into manors. Each one had its own tenants, and there was seldom room for any new ones. There was no work by which one could earn his bread. For a long while there was only one way by which a boy could escape from the manor life, and that was by becoming a priest. If he wished to be a priest, and showed that he had the ability, his lord had to let him go free.

Farm work was exceedingly hard in those days, for the implements were rude and clumsy. The ploughs, for instance, were made of wood and were so heavy that eight oxen were needed to draw them. The manor life could not have been very agreeable,

A SCENE IN A NORMAN HALL
Evelyn Paul

but it had one great advantage, it was safe, for the lord was bound to protect his tenants, and in those days of strife and disorder it was a great thing to have protection. Indeed, it often happened that, for the sake of being protected a free man would go of his own accord to some powerful noble and offer to become his vassal.

Between the eleventh and the thirteenth centuries, many knights went on crusades, or warlike expeditions to try to rescue the Holy Land from the Mohammedans. These knights required large sums of money, and they allowed many of their tenants to pay their rent in money instead of work. Sometimes they would even let them have a piece of land. This made the villeins feel a little more independent; but until after the battles of Crécy and Poitiers it did not occur to them that they were well able to protect themselves with their own weapons. They had supposed that to be an efficient soldier it was necessary to have a horse and armour, and to be trained as a knight; but these two battles were won by men who had no armour and no swords, but only their bows and arrows.

Two or three years after the battle of Crécy, a terrible disease known as the Black Death swept over the land. So many villeins died that now a man could find plenty of work at good wages wherever he chose to go. Moreover, if he did not wish to work on a manor, he could live in a city if he chose, for fine wool weaving had been introduced from Flanders and he could easily earn his living as a weaver.

Thus, little by little the old way of living on manors was given up, and the feudal system gradually disappeared. In a few places in Europe, however, the ground is still cultivated in great fields wherein each person holds one or more strips; and in the little town of Manheim, in Pennsylvania, there is some land that is held by a sort of feudal tenure. It was given by a wealthy baron a century and a half ago as a site for a church, and the rental was to be, as in the case of the land in Newcastle, "one red rose, payable in June, when the same shall be lawfully demanded." Twice the baron asked for the rose, and then the old custom was forgotten until it was revived a few years ago. Now one day in every June is set apart for the payment of the rose to some descendant of the baron. There is always a pleasant little celebration. Then, after the music and the addresses in the church, the people present all walk past the chancel, each one laying down a red rose as he passes. The roses are afterward gathered up and carried to the sick folk in some hospital.

CHAPTER XXV

TOWN LIFE IN THE MIDDLE AGES

P EOPLE living in a town in the Middle Ages had to make sure that it could not be easily captured by an enemy. For this reason they often built a heavy wall around it with watch-towers where men were always on guard. Battering-rams and other machines for knocking down a wall could not be used unless they were brought close up to it, and therefore just outside the fortifications of the city a deep ditch was often dug and kept full of water. There were only a few gates, and those were carefully protected. Outside the walls were forests and fields, and every morning the public herdsman drove the oxen of the townspeople to pasture, bringing them back again at night. There were gardens and cultivated fields around the town; and indeed there were many gardens and orchards within the walls. If everything had been kept clean, a town might have been a pleasant, sweet-smelling place; but rubbish was heaped up in front of the doors, and pigs roamed about the streets at their own will. These streets were usually narrow and crooked.

There were no pavements, and the upper stories of the houses sometimes projected so far that people living on opposite sides of a street could shake hands from their windows.

The nearer one came to the centre of the town, the closer together were the houses. Mer-

AN OLD STREET
(In the town of Dijon, France)

chants usually had shop and home in the same building. The lower part of the front was the shop, and the rear of the house was the home. This was by far the pleasanter part, for it often looked out upon gardens filled with bright flowers.

Besides the merchants, there were the humbler folk, the craftsmen, that is, the carpenters, masons, black-smiths, and others. Every trade had its apprentices, boys who were bound to remain with some craftsman a certain number of years to learn his business. The master fed and clothed the boy, gave him a home, and taught him. When he had finished his apprenticeship, he became a journey-man, or workman. Of course he was eager to become a master, but before he could do this, he must make a "masterpiece," that is, a piece of work excellent enough to be accepted by the guild or soci-ety composed of the men of his trade.

There were guilds of bakers, weavers, coopers, brewers, goldsmiths, carpenters; indeed, every trade had its guild. The guild did a great deal for its members. If one of them became poor or was ill, his guild gave him assistance. If he died in poverty, the guild paid his funeral expenses and aided his family. If a journey-man, a cooper, for instance, came to a strange town, the guild of coopers in that town would find work for him; or, if there was none, they would give him money to pay his way to the next town.

OLD TOWN
IN LOCHES,
FRANCE
(Built in the
Middle Ages)

The guild not only helped its members, but saw to it that they did not impose upon the public. If a baker made his loaves too small or a dyer gave short measure of cloth or a maker of spurs gilded old ones and sold them for new, his guild punished him by a fine or by expulsion. The master himself was punished, and not the workman who had, perhaps, done the actual work. In many places men were forbidden by their guilds to carry on their trades after the curfew bell, lest they should not do good work, or should disturb their neighbours, or perhaps set their houses ablaze.

The craft guilds were also religious societies, and each one had its patron saint. They gave altars and painted windows and generous presents of money to the cathedrals. The whole guild often went to church in solemn procession. They also presented

153

what were known as mystery plays, that is, plays showing forth scenes in the Bible. One guild presented the creation of the world, another the flood, another the flight of the Holy Family into Egypt, and so on.

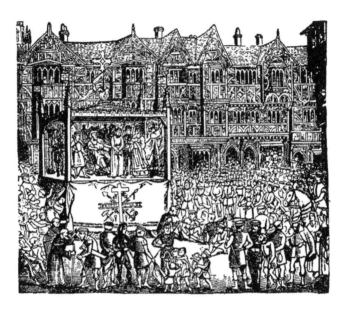

A MYSTERY PLAY OF THE MIDDLE AGES

The presenting of these plays was often very expensive, but it was looked upon as a religious duty. When the morning for the plays had come, the members of the guild met together, and after prayers those who were to act clambered into a clumsy two-story wagon called a pageant, and went to the corner or open square where the play was to be shown. When it was enacted, they moved on to present the same play elsewhere, while another guild acted the second play of the series in the place that they had just left. When the play had been repeated in all the places chosen, the members of the guilds went to their homes, feeling that they had performed a religious duty that would be good for them and for the crowds that had been listening to them.

Another later kind was known as a morality play, in which characters representing the virtues and vices took part. The incidents in these plays were not drawn directly from the Bible, as was the case with the mystery plays. Ultimately this rude acting developed into the great Elizabethan drama.

The merchants, too, had their guilds, and these were very powerful associations. They won a great deal of liberty for the towns; for when a king or noble was in need of money, the rich merchant guilds would say, "We will provide it if you will agree no longer to lay taxes upon our town at your own will." Sometimes the guilds made rather hard bargains. If a king or a nobleman wished to go on a crusade, or if he had been taken prisoner and needed a large sum of money for his ransom, he was ready to give many privileges to the town that would supply him with gold, or even to grant it the right to govern itself in all things. Many a city literally bought its charter with its gold.

These merchant guilds were afterwards called corporations, and from them was gradually developed the Town Council of the present day.

CHAPTER XXVI

PETER THE HERMIT LEADS THE FIRST CRUSADE

D URING many centuries, if a man asked, "What can I do that will be most pleasing to God?" not only the priests but nearly all his friends would answer, "Make a pilgrimage to Jerusalem, to the place where our Lord suffered and was buried." To go from England or any part of Western Europe was a long journey, and often dangerous, but it was not expensive, for all Christians felt it a duty to give the pilgrims food and lodging. Jerusalem was in the hands of the Saracens. They were Mohammedans, but they had no objection to allowing pilgrims to visit the city, especially as the wealthier among them spent much money during their stay. Good Harun-al-Raschid even erected a Christian church and a building in which the pilgrims might lodge.

About the time that William the Conqueror took possession of England, the Seljukian Turks captured Jerusalem. Then it became a different matter to make a pilgrimage to the Holy City, for the pilgrims were robbed and tortured and sometimes put to death. The Emperor in the East and the popes, one after another, were most indignant. Finally Pope Urban II. determined that the church should be aroused to capture the Holy Land from the Turks. He had a powerful helper, a Frenchman known as Peter the Hermit. Peter had been on a

PETER THE HERMIT PREACHING

pilgrimage to the Holy Land, and on his return he travelled about Europe in coarse woollen shirt and hermit's cloak, telling people everywhere of the cruelties of the Turks. At Clermont in France, Pope Urban went out into a wide-spreading plain and made an eloquent address to the thousands of Frenchmen who were gathered together. He told

157

them that God had given their nation glory in arms, and that He wished them to use their power, not in fighting with one another, but in winning the city of Christ from the infidels. The multitude shouted, "God wills it! God wills it!" and it was not long before hundreds of thousands had fastened the red cross to their shoulders and had set out for Jerusalem. The Latin word for cross is *crux*, and from this the expedition was known as a crusade. The pope had urged that none should go unless they were able to bear arms, and that the rich should take soldiers with them; but people paid little attention to this advice.

The first company started under Peter the Hermit and a knight known as Walter the Penniless. Not all its members, however, were real pilgrims. Some went for gain, some to see the world, and some were mere robbers and thieves. Peter had no authority over them, and they did what they chose. While they were passing through Germany, the people were kind to them and gladly brought them food; but when they came to other countries, they were not treated so generously. Then they demanded food, often most insolently, and when it was refused, they stole it. They killed flocks and herds and even their owners. Of course the people avenged their wrongs with the sword. The pilgrims fought or fled as best they might. On arriving at Constantinople they were received kindly by the emperor and given food; but even there they stole from houses and gardens and churches. They pushed on toward

Jerusalem, and soon were attacked and slaughtered by the Turks.

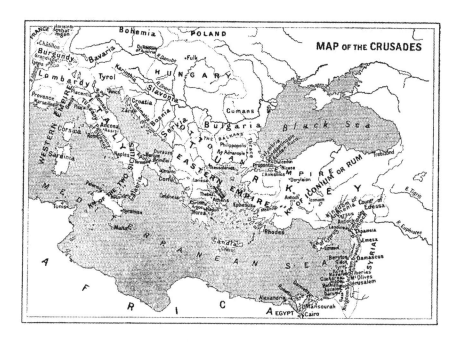

But there were hundreds of thousands of others making ready to join the crusade who were not wild, turbulent folk like the first company, but were far more earnest and serious. It is thought that at least 100,000 of these were knights. They came by different ways, but all met at Constantinople. Then they marched on into Asia Minor. They were in need of food and even of water. Thousands perished. The others were saved by some dogs that had followed them. These dogs deserted their masters, but finally came back to the camp. "See their muddy paws! They have found water!" cried the thirsty people. They followed the dogs' tracks and came to water. A pigeon, too, did them a good turn. One ruler had pretended to be friendly, but just after they had left his territory, they picked up in their camp a dead carrier pigeon, bearing a letter to the ruler of the next district, bidding him destroy "the accursed Christians."

THE ARRIVAL OF THE CRUSADERS AT JERUSALEM

So they went on; sometimes they captured a town; sometimes many of them died of famine or plague. At length they came in sight of the Holy City, and then all their troubles were forgotten. They cried, "Jerusalem! Jerusalem!" They fell upon their knees, they kissed one another with joy, they cast off their shoes, for had not the very soil become holy

THE STORMING OF JERUSALEM

where the Lord had once walked? They threw themselves down upon it and kissed the ground. With shouts of "God wills it! God wills it!" they attacked the walls. After a savage combat, the city was captured. Then came a massacre of Saracens as brutal as any in history; for even the gallant knights had not yet learned that it is better to convert an enemy than to kill him.

CHURCH OF THE HOLY SEPULCHRE, JERUSALEM

The most valiant leader among the crusaders was Godfrey of Bouillon, and he was chosen king of what was called the Kingdom of Jerusalem. He was escorted to the Church of the Holy Sepulchre, and there he would have been crowned, but he said, "No, I cannot wear a crown of gold in the very city in which my Lord and Master wore a crown of thorns." He was willing to be called Defender of the

Holy Sepulchre, but he would not take the title of king.

Godfrey and a few other knights remained in Jerusalem, and the rest of the pilgrims went to their homes. They had spent four years in this crusade; hundreds of thousands of Christians, and perhaps as many Saracens, had been slain; but the Holy City had been taken from the infidels, and there was great rejoicing.

CHAPTER XXVII

RICHARD THE LION-HEARTED

THERE were several expeditions to rescue Jerusalem, but the third may fairly be named the Royal Crusade because of the number of sovereigns who took part in it. There was Frederick, the German Emperor, nicknamed Barbarossa because of his long red beard; there was Philip II., King of France; and there was Richard I. of England, the famous Cœur de Lion, the lion-hearted soldier.

After being eighty-eight years in the hands of the Christians, Jerusalem had been recaptured in 1187 by a great Saracen commander named Saladin. He was far more merciful, however, than the Christians of the first crusade, for when the women of Jerusalem begged for the lives of their fathers and brothers and husbands, he forgot all his stern threats and not only freed his prisoners, but loaded them with presents.

The Emperor Frederick could not bear the thought of Jerusalem being in the hands of the Saracens, and he set off with his army to regain it. He was a brave and wise soldier and would have led his troops most nobly, but by some accident he was drowned before reaching the Holy Land. His subjects were heartbroken at the news of his death. They could hardly believe it possible, and the legend arose that he had hidden himself away in the depths of the mountains; and fathers said to their children, "The good Barbarossa is not dead. He and his daughter and his brave comrades sit about a marble table in some mountain cavern. His red beard has grown through the marble, so long has

FREDERICK
BARBAROSSA

he waited. But by and by there will come a time when the ravens no longer fly around the mountain. Then he will come forth, and in that day our land shall be great indeed."

King Richard of England was eager for glory and would gladly have set out for the Holy Land at once; but first the money for an army must be raised. How it was raised he did not care. More than one man who wanted to be a bishop, obtained his wish by paying for it. If a man was guilty of wrong-doing, he need not go to prison if he could send a goodly sum of money to the king. England held two fortresses in Scotland; but Richard willingly gave up all claim to them and to the whole country for ten thousand marks. He and Philip Augustus of France were enemies, but now they swore to be most faithful friends. "If one of us is slain during the crusade," they said, "the other shall take all troops and money

165

and go on with the great work of freeing the Holy Land." Richard meant to have better order than during the first crusade, and he made some remarkable laws. If one man killed another, the murderer was to be tied to the body of his victim, and both were to be thrown into the sea. A man who stole was to have hot pitch poured upon his head and over this feathers were to be shaken.

At length both French and English were on the way; but long before they reached Syria, the two kings quarrelled. They patched up a sort of peace and went on to Acre, a seaport town of Syria that the Christians were besieging. That soon fell. Both kings put their banners on the ramparts; but Richard took up his abode in the royal palace, leaving to Philip a humbler place. Indeed, in whatever they did, Richard always took the first place; and before long Philip declared that he was sick and should return to Europe. "If you are really sick or afraid of the enemy, you would better go home," said Richard scornfully. He easily guessed that Philip's real reason for wishing to go home was that he might try to seize some of the English possessions, and he made the French king swear not to make war upon any of the English lands while he himself was away.

Richard marched south toward Jerusalem. Every night when he halted, heralds cried three times, "Save the Holy Sepulchre!" and all the army knelt and said "Amen!" The hot-tempered Richard had already had trouble, not only with Philip but with Duke Leopold of Austria; for at Acre the duke

RICHARD AND PHILIP AT THE SIEGE OF ACRE

had set his banner upon a tower that he had taken, and Richard had torn it down and flung it into the ditch. There was also trouble at Ascalon. Richard was bent upon rebuilding the walls. With his own royal hands he brought stones and mortar. Leopold refused to follow his example, and he declared as the old poem puts it,—

> "My father n'as mason ne carpenter;
>   And though your walls should all to shake,
>   I shall never help hem to make."

Then, as the story goes, Richard not only stormed at the noble duke, but struck him. Naturally, the duke too went home.

On the whole, none of the warriors seems to have behaved in so praiseworthy a fashion as the Mohammedan Saladin. This brave and knightly leader greatly admired the daring deeds of Richard. They exchanged many courtesies, and when the English king was ill, his enemy sent him fruit and ice for his comfort.

Richard's boldness amazed every one. He was always in the thickest of the fight, striking off a foeman's head with one blow of his sword, or swinging his terrible battle-axe with twenty pounds of steel in its head. One of his enemies declared, "No man can escape from his sword; his attack is dreadful; to engage with him is fatal, and his deeds are beyond human nature." Saladin's brother, too, looked upon his enemy with warmest admiration; and when Richard was once dismounted in battle, the Saracen sent him as a gift two noble horses. It is said that fifty years later, if the horse of a Saracen shied, his rider would say, "What, do you think you see King Richard in that bush?"

KING RICHARD IN COMBAT

But the Germans and the French, and even many of his own troops, had left Richard. Therefore, as he had not men enough to take Jerusalem, he made the best terms he could with Saladin and departed from the Holy Land. On the way home overland through Austria he was captured by his enemy, Duke Leopold, given over to the Emperor of Germany, and put into prison. There is a pleasant story that Blondel, one of his minstrels, roamed over Europe in search of his beloved master. A minstrel might go safely wherever he would, and Blondel wandered about for a year without success. At last some country folk pointed out a castle belonging to the emperor and said, "Folk say there is a king kept prisoner in that tower." Then Blondel sang beside the tower the first stanza of a little French song that he and the king had written together. He paused a moment, and from the tower came the voice of Richard singing the second stanza. Blondel straightway went home and told the English where their king was, and they were ready to pay ransom for him. Philip of France and Richard's younger brother John—the John who had to sign Magna Charta some years later—did all they could to have him kept in prison; for Philip thought he could seize Normandy if Richard was out of the way. As for John, he had been ruling England during his brother's absence, and he was determined not to give up the kingdom. But the pope threatened Philip and the emperor with excommunication from the church if they did not let Richard go; and at last they yielded. It was not easy to raise the large ransom demanded, but the English had a hearty admiration for their king, and finally it was paid and Richard was set free.

He hastened to England, and the whole English people rejoiced, save John and his followers. To John, Philip had sent a message saying, "Take care of yourself; the devil has broken loose." Richard, however, made no attempt to punish his brother, and even when John again showed himself unfaithful, Richard forgave him, saying, "I hope I shall as easily forget his injuries as he will my pardon."

CHAPTER XXVIII

THE CHILDREN'S CRUSADE

A MARVELLOUS thing now came to pass, for the children of France and Germany went on a crusade. Stephen, a French shepherd boy twelve years old, declared that Jesus had appeared to him and bidden him lead a company of children to rescue the Holy Sepulchre from the infidels. Other children joined him, and they went about from village to village, bearing crosses and candles, swinging censers, singing hymns, and crying, "God wills it! God wills it!" Soon a great army of boys and girls, including the humblest shepherd lads and the children of wealthy nobles, started to march for the Holy Land. No one could stop them. The king bade them return to their homes, but they only cried the more, "God wills it!" They broke away from their friends, from the very arms of their parents. The older folk knew not what to think. Some said this was a work of Satan to destroy the children. Others believed that it was the will of God that where armed men had failed, innocent children should succeed; and they dared not hold them back lest they should be fighting against God.

THE CHILDREN CROSSING THE ALPS

In Germany, too, there was a boy preacher, one Nicholas; and he aroused the German children as Stephen aroused the French. The little German boys and girls set out, twenty thousand strong, many of them wearing long grey coats upon which crosses were sewn. They had broad-brimmed hats, and they carried the staffs of pilgrims. As they marched, they sang hymns. One of these has come down to us. It begins,

> *Fairest Lord Jesus,*
> *Ruler of all nature.*

But the way grew rougher and rougher. The air of the mountains was cold. They came to desert places where there was no food. Thousands died, and when the others reached the city of Genoa, they were only seven thousand. Still the children did not lose courage. God would open a way for them through the sea, they believed, and soon they would be in the Holy Land. They would tell the story of the good Jesus. The infidels would listen and would become His followers.

The morning came. They waited patiently on the shore at Genoa, but no path was opened through the sea. There is a tradition that part of the children sailed for Syria, but what became of them is not known. Some pressed on to Rome. They told the Pope about their journey and their sufferings. He said that it was of no use for them to try to reach

Syria, but, as they were bound by their vows, they must go on a crusade when they were older.

By this time only a few children were left. Many had died, as has been said; some had been stolen or sold as slaves, and still others had stopped in one place or another. Nothing now remained but to suffer the long, hard journey home; and at last this, too, was ended. "Tell us of your wanderings. Where have you been?" begged their parents and friends; but all that the tired little crusaders could answer was, "We do not know."

Meanwhile, the French children, thirty thousand in all, had set out for Marseilles. Their way was less rough, but the heat of the summer was terrible. Many of the little ones had never been farther from their homes than some neighbouring village, and whenever they came in sight of a city wall or a castle, they would ask piteously, "Isn't that Jerusalem?" After a journey of three hundred miles, about twenty thousand of them came to Marseilles. "Let us stay here to-night," they begged, "and to-morrow God will open a way for us through the sea." No path was opened, and many started to return to their homes. At length two merchants offered to provide vessels for all who wished to go to the Holy Land. "We do it for the cause of God," they said, "and we ask no reward but your prayers." Then the children were happy. "This is the path through the sea," they cried joyfully. "This is what God promised us." Seven vessels full of the bravest of the children set sail to cross the blue Mediterranean. Eighteen years later, an old priest came to Europe, and told the sad ending of the story. Two of the seven vessels had been wrecked; but the hundreds of children on board the others had been carried to the coast of Africa and sold to the Mohammedans as slaves; for the generous men of Marseilles who had so kindly offered to carry them across the sea were slave traders. Not one of the seven shiploads of children ever saw his home again.

CHAPTER XXIX

ROGER BACON

WHILST the thirteenth century was by no means free from wars, the Western nations of Europe were beginning to feel the results of ordered government, and a great impetus was given to intellectual pursuits. To a very great extent this took the direction of theological disputes, but secular knowledge also shared the inspiration.

The scientists of that day were concerned almost solely with astrology and alchemy, and owing to the superstition then so prevalent, all who studied these so-called sciences were liable to be suspected of practising the magic arts.

Roger Bacon was not the man to be turned from the pursuit of knowledge, by any fear of evil consequences that might spring from the ignorance of his fellow-men. Born of a good Somerset family, he was sent to Oxford, where he studied the works of Aristotle, which had been forgotten for centuries, and thus became acquainted with the greatest of the classical scientists. He also took a great interest in mathematics, and was the first to apply this knowledge to the science of astronomy. After some years

at Oxford, he went to the University of Paris, returning to Oxford again in 1250. He then entered the
Franciscan Order, and hence is often called Friar
Bacon. Having acquired all the learning of the age,
he spent all that he had, and much that he borrowed
from friends, in his scientific researches into the
secrets of nature. He was especially interested in the
science of optics, as being useful to the study of
astronomy, and this resulted in the invention of the
magnifying glass, but he was greatly hindered by the
need of proper apparatus.

Such a man would naturally gather many students around him, and we learn that he was a kindly
teacher, and never hesitated to impart his knowledge
freely, when his scholars were too poor to make him
any payment.

"From my youth up," he writes, "I have
laboured at the sciences and tongues. I have sought
the friendship of all men among the Latins who had
any reputation for knowledge. I have caused youths
to be instructed in languages, geometry, arithmetic,
the construction of tables and instruments, and
many needful things besides."

Returning to Paris, his great gifts brought him
many enemies, and he was at last accused of the
practice of magic and imprisoned in 1257. He was
forbidden all intercourse with the world, and even
the privilege of writing was denied him. Then Pope
Clement IV. became interested in his work, and it
was at the Pope's request that Bacon wrote his *Opus
Magus*, and the manuscript was sent to Rome by *the*

THE WIZARD
Sir E. Burne-Jones

hand of his favourite pupil, John of London. We do not know how it was received, for Clement died shortly afterward.

This wonderful book sums up the state of knowledge, both in philosophy and science, of the time. Many other books were written by Friar Bacon, some of which have never been translated from the Latin in which all learned books were written in his day, for Latin was still the common language of European scholars.

In his later years Bacon drew up a rectified calendar, invented gunpowder, and was, as Mr. Lecky says, "the greatest natural philosopher of the Middle Ages." It seems strange to us that such a man could believe in astrology and in the philosopher's stone, but Bacon was sufficiently a child of his time to feel the fascination which these idle pursuits had for nearly all the learned men of that day.

Bacon's greatest achievement was his application of new principles to the study of science. He believed that experiment was necessary, and not merely the acceptance of beliefs handed down from ancient philosophers. To his optical and astronomical researches he brought to bear his knowledge of mathematics, in which he had learnt much from the Arabs, who in that day were especially renowned in that science.

Although his work had no great immediate effect, owing to the decay of *learning* during the next two centuries, when all the energies of the Church were devoted to preventing schism, his influence during the Renaissance in the sixteenth century was marked, for many of his books were amongst the earliest printed.

Bacon was released from prison in Paris about the year 1267, and for ten years enjoyed his freedom in spite of the attacks of his enemies. In 1278 the chief of the Franciscan Order declared his books to be unorthodox, and kept him in confinement until 1292. Two years later he died at Oxford.

CHAPTER XXX

MARCO POLO

IN the days of Marco Polo, Venice was one of the richest and most powerful cities in Europe, and nowhere else, perhaps, could one see so many magnificent palaces and churches. Venice had shrewd merchants, daring sailors, and many ships, and it was chiefly through the enormous trade which she had built up with the East that she had grown so wealthy.

Among the most enterprising of the Venetian merchants were the father and uncle of Marco Polo. Indeed, when Marco was a little boy, he used to hear stories of his father and his uncle that must have seemed to him almost like fairy tales. "They went away from Venice to make a voyage to Constantinople," the little boy's friends said, "and in Constantinople they bought a great quantity of rich jewelry. We think they must have gone into the unknown countries of Asia to trade, perhaps even to China, where the great khan lives."

When the boy was about fourteen, his father came home, and then he had stories to tell indeed. He had gone far into Asia, had sold the jewelry brought from Constantinople, had been at the court of the great Kublai Khan, ruler of China, and now he and his brother had come back to Italy with a message from the khan to the Pope. He showed the boy the khan's golden tablets which he had given to the brothers. The royal cipher was engraved upon them and a command that wherever in the khan's domain the brothers might go, his subjects should receive them with honour and should provide them with whatever they needed. The brothers were going back to China, and now the boy was happy, for his father promised that he might go with them.

Then they made the long, leisurely journey from Venice to Constantinople, and across Asia to China. They travelled through fertile valleys and sandy deserts, over stony mountains and through gloomy passes. They saw strange birds and fruits and peoples. They visited handsome cities, and lonely tribes that had no settled homes. It was a slow journey. In one place the sickness of the young Marco delayed them for many months. Sometimes they had to wait for company before they could venture through dangerous countries. Once they had to go far out of their way to avoid passing through a region where two tribes were waging war. At length they came within forty miles of the home of the great Kublai Khan, ruler of China. Here they were met by a large escort, sent out by the khan, and were brought into the city with every mark of honour that could be shown them.

The khan took a strong liking to the young Marco, and gave him a position in the royal household. The young man put on the Chinese dress, adopted the Chinese manners and customs and learned the four languages that were most used in the country. The khan was delighted with him and often gave him a golden tablet and sent him off on a journey so that on his return he could describe to him the wonderful things that he had seen. Marco's father and uncle were also given positions in the khan's service, and by his generosity they soon became exceedingly wealthy.

China was not home, however, even after they had lived in that country for many years, and they longed to see their own Venice. They begged the khan to allow them to return. "But why?" he asked. "It is a dangerous journey; you might lose your lives. Do you want money or jewels? I will give you twice as much as you now have; but I care for you too much to let you go away from me." Without the khan's tablets, the journey would be impossible; and the Polos began to fear they would never see their home again.

Some months before this the ruler of Persia had sent an embassy to beg that a granddaughter of the Great Khan might become his wife. The princess and her suite set off for Persia; but the way lay through a country that was at war, and they had to return. The Persian ambassadors, however, had been away from Persia three years, and they did not dare to remain longer at the Chinese court. Just then, Marco Polo arrived from a voyage to some of the islands off the coast. The idea occurred to the ambassadors that they might take ship and go by water to the Persian Gulf at less expense and with greater safety than by the overland way. They talked with the Polos, and found that they would be only too glad to go with them. Then they begged the khan to allow the three Venetians, who were experienced sailors, to escort them. The khan was not pleased, but he finally yielded. He gave the Polos his golden tablets, loaded them down with presents of jewels, and they and the ambassadors and the fair young princess sailed away with a fleet of fourteen vessels furnished with stores and provisions for two years. It was twenty-one months before they came to Persia. The Polos rested a year in the leisurely fashion of those days, then returned, not to China, but to Venice, having been absent twenty-four years.

At Venice there had been rumors long before that the famous travelers were dead. They were, of course, greatly changed, and they spoke Italian rather stiffly and queerly. It was hard to believe that these foreign-looking men in their long, rough Tartar coats could be the members of the wealthy family of Polo. They had some trouble in getting possession

MARCO POLO'S RETURN

of their own palace, and even after they had succeeded, many thought they were impostors. The story is told that to convince these doubting friends, they invited them to a magnificent banquet. After the feast, the coarse, threadbare coats were brought in and quickly ripped open. There rolled out such a store of rubies and emeralds and diamonds and sapphires as the bewildered guests had never seen. The whole room blazed and sparkled with them. For the sake of safety on the dangerous journey, the Polos had brought their immense wealth in this form. Then the guests were convinced that the three men were not impostors, and they were treated with the utmost respect.

War broke out between Venice and Genoa, and Marco Polo was put in command of a warship. He was taken prisoner by the Genoese and it was while he was in prison that he dictated to a gentleman of Genoa the stories of his travels. All Genoa became interested, and their famous prisoner was soon set free. Copies of his book in manuscript went everywhere. Some doubted its truth, and when the author was on his deathbed, they begged him to take back the parts of it that they thought must be exaggerated. "There is no exaggeration in the book," he declared. "On the contrary, I have not told half the amazing things that I saw with my own eyes."

CHAPTER XXXI

FRANCESCO PETRARCH

HUNDREDS of thousands of men returned from the crusades with their minds full of new ideas. They had seen the distant countries of the East with their mountains, rivers, plains, and seas. In the great cities they had gazed upon hundreds of handsome buildings different from anything in their own lands. Many of the French, German, and English crusaders had gone to Venice to take ship to cross the Mediterranean, and there they had seen most superb structures of coloured marble. The outside of the Venetian palaces was generally adorned with bas-relief, and the groundwork was often coloured a deep, rich blue, while the sculpture was covered with gold leaf. Moreover, the crusaders had learned that their own ways of living were not always the best and most comfortable. They had found that there were kinds of food and materials for clothing better than those to which they had been accustomed; that there were beautiful furnishings for houses of which they had never dreamed. Having seen such things or heard of them, people wished to buy them. The cities about the

Adriatic Sea, especially Venice and Genoa, were ready to supply all these newly discovered needs. Long before this, the Venetians had driven the pirates from the Adriatic and had claimed the sea as their own. To symbolize this victory, they had a poetical custom. Every Ascension Day the doge, or ruler of the city, sailed out in a vessel most magnificently decorated, and with a vast amount of ceremony dropped a golden ring into the water to indicate that the city had become the bride of the

THE CEREMONY OF MAKING VENICE
THE "BRIDE OF THE SEA."

sea. Venice had built ships and carried the armies of crusaders across the water. She had gained stations on the eastern shore of the Adriatic, and might fairly claim to rule the whole sea. She had used her ships for other purposes, however, than carrying armies, for she had an enormous trade, as we have said, in the beautiful things that were made in the distant lands of the East. She brought home cargoes of rich tapestries and silks, jewels, glassware, and most exquisite pieces of work in iron and gold and enamel. Her workmen copied them and found in them hints and suggestions for other work. These things were carried over Europe, and even to far-away England.

The crusades not only taught people about other lands and other customs, but they taught them to wish to see more of the world, to know what men of other countries were doing and thinking. People began to have more interest in what was written in books. They had thought that a man encased in armour, carrying a sword and a lance, and set upon a horse, was the ideal hero. Now they began to have a glimmering idea that the man who had noble thoughts and could put them into noble words was greater than the man with the sword.

The most famous scholar of the age was an Italian poet called Petrarch. Even as a boy he loved the writings of the early Latin and Greek authors. His father wished him to become a lawyer, and the boy listened to some lectures on law; but all the while he was saving his money to buy the works of Cicero and Virgil. His father threw the precious manuscripts into the fire; but when he saw the grief of the boy, he snatched them out again. Thus Petrarch slowly won his way to being a poet and scholar. He became a great collector of manuscripts, especially of the Greek and Roman writers; and, moreover, he showed people how to study them. Before his day, even students had felt that if two copies of an author's work did not agree, one was as likely to be correct as the other. Petrarch taught people to compare manuscripts, to study them, and so learn whether one was copied from another, or whether those in existence had all been copied from some older writing that was lost.

Princes and other great men of Italy admired his poetry and showed him much respect, but there

were two special honours for which he longed. One was to be crowned as poet by the Roman senate; the other was to wear a similar crown in Paris. On one happy September day invitations to receive both these crowns came to him. He had always taught that it was wrong for a man not to make the most of himself, and even when he was seventy, he did not think of giving up work. His physicians said, "You must rest"; but, instead of resting, he engaged five or six secretaries and worked as hard as ever. One morning he was found in his library, his head lying on an open book. He was dead.

PETRARCH
(From an old painting)

His influence, however, did not die. Others, too, began to collect the long-forgotten manuscripts of the Greek and Roman authors. They searched monasteries and churches and made many copies of the precious writings. Italy was all alive with interest in the great works of the ancient writers. The Italian students thought wistfully of the manuscripts that must be stored away in Greece. They did not know how soon they would be able to read them for themselves and without leaving their own country.

Thus it was that, although the crusaders did not win Jerusalem and though the Holy City is even to-day in the hands of the Mohammedans, yet the crusades did much to encourage commerce, to give people new ideas on many subjects, and to prepare them to receive the knowledge that was coming to them slowly from the East.

CHAPTER XXXII

THE FALL OF CONSTANTINOPLE

W HILE the Italian scholars were wishing that they had more of the precious old manuscripts, there were exciting times in the country known as Turkey in Europe. This country had been part of the Eastern Empire even after the fall of Rome in 476, but it had come to be so little Roman and so completely Greek that it is spoken of as the Greek, or Byzantine Empire. It was destined, however, to belong to neither Romans nor Greeks, for the Mohammedans were pressing hard upon its boundaries. They had won Asia Minor and the lands lying directly south of the Danube. Gradually they got Greece, north of the Isthmus, into their power, and in 1453 Mohammed II. led the Ottoman Turks, who were of the same race as Attila and his Huns, against the capital of the Eastern Empire, the great rich city of Constantinople.

Gunpowder had been invented before this time, but the cannon were small. When the great Turkish gun fired its heavy stone balls, men and women rushed into the streets, beating their breasts and crying aloud, "God have mercy upon us!" Day after day the besiegers continued the attack. They used arrows, and catapults for throwing stones. They wheeled a two-story tower covered with hides near enough to the city so that archers in the second story could shoot at the defenders on the walls. But the Greeks threw their famous Greek fire upon it and it was consumed. Both parties dug mines. Sometimes these were blown up, sometimes the workers in them were suffocated by smoke or gas.

ST. SOPHIA, CONSTANTINOPLE
(The famous church built in the 6th century by the emperor Justinian. It has been used as a mosque since the capture of Constantinople by the Turks)

Finally the Turks dug a narrow canal five miles long from the Sea of Marmora to the harbor of Constantinople. They paved it with beams, well greased, and one morning the Greeks found thirty Turkish ships lying almost under their walls, for the oxen of the Turks had dragged them to the shore during the night. Then the people of the city were in despair and begged their emperor to escape and flee for his life, but he refused. "I am resolved to die here with you," he declared.

When it was seen that the city must fall, thousands of the citizens crowded into the vast church of St. Sophia, for there was an old prophecy that some day the Turks would force their way into the city, but that when they had reached St. Sophia an angel would appear with a celestial sword, and that at sight of it the Turks would flee. The emperor knelt long in prayer, received the Holy Communion, and then begged the priests and all the members of his court to forgive him if he had ever wronged them. The sobs and wails of the people echoed in the great building.

The Turks made their way without hindrance into the city. They did not stop at the church; and no angel brought a miraculous weapon to drive them back. The emperor fell, sword in hand, fighting to the last for his empire and the Christian faith. The Turkish commander gave over the city to his soldiers, and they stole everything worth stealing,— wonderful treasures of gold, silver, bronze, and jewels. Thousands of citizens were roughly bound together and dragged off to the boats to be sold as slaves. The cross was torn down from beautiful St. Sophia, and the crescent, the emblem of Mohammedanism, was put in its place.

The emperor's body, however, was buried by the Turks with all honour. A lamp was lighted at his grave. It is still kept burning, and at the charge of the Turkish government. This was commanded by the Turkish ruler as a mark of respect and regard for Constantine Palæologos, the last Christian emperor in the Empire of the East.

At the coming of the Turks, many of the Greeks had seized their most valued treasures and fled. The scholars carried away with them the rare old manuscripts of the early Greek writers. More went to Italy than anywhere else, and the Italian scholars gave them a hearty welcome. There had been learned Greeks in Italy long before this time, and the Italian scholars had been interested in the Greek literature; but now such a wealth of it was poured into the country that the Italians were aroused and delighted. They read the manuscripts eagerly; they sent copies to their friends; and gradually a knowledge of the literature of the Greeks and a love for it spread throughout Europe.

CHAPTER XXXIII

JOHN GUTENBERG

T HE fall of Constantinople had brought the Greek scholars with their manuscripts to Italy, but it would have been a long while before even the most learned men of Western Europe could have read the writings had not a Ger-man named John Guten-berg been working away for many years, trying to invent a better process of making books than the slow, tiresome method of copying them by hand, letter by letter. When Gutenberg was a boy, this was the way in which all books were made. More-over, they were generally written on parchment, and this added to the expense. The result was that a book was a costly article, and few people could afford to own one. When Guten-

MONK WRITING
MANUSCRIPT

berg became a young man, a way of making books was invented which people thought was a most wonderful improvement. For each page the printer took a block of fine-grained wood, drew upon it whatever picture he was to print, then cut the wood away, leaving the outlines of the picture. By inking this and pressing it upon the paper he could print a page. Only one side of the paper was used, and so every pair of leaves had to be pasted together. At first only pictures were printed, but after a while some lettering was also done. Such books were called block books. Many were printed in this way with pictures illustrating Bible history; and these were known as poor men's Bibles.

Although the block books were much less expensive than the books written by hand, still they were by no means cheap. It was long, slow work to cut a block for each page; and after as many books had been printed as were needed, the blocks were of no further use. Gutenberg wondered whether there was not some better way to print a book. He pondered and dreamed over the matter and made experiments. At last the idea which he sought came to him, an idea so simple that it seems strange no one had thought of it sooner. It was only to cut each letter on a separate piece of wood, form the letters into words, bind them together the shape and size of a page, print as many copies as were desired, then separate the letters and use them in other books till they were worn out. Here was the great invention; but it was a long way from this beginning to a well-printed book.

Now people began to wonder what Gutenberg could be working at so secretly. In those days everything that was mysterious was thought to be witchcraft; so the inventor, in order to avoid any such charge, made himself a workshop in a deserted monastery outside of the town. He had yet to learn how to make his types of metal, how to fasten them together firmly in forms, how to put on just enough ink, and how to make a press.

GUTENBERG'S HOUSE
(At Strasburg, Germany)

At length he carried through a great undertaking,—he printed a Latin Bible. This was completed in 1455, and was the first Bible ever printed. But Gutenberg was in trouble. He had not had the money needed to carry on this work without help, and he had been obliged to take a partner by the name of John Faust. Faust was disappointed in not making as much money as he had expected. The Bible had taken longer to complete and had cost more than Gutenberg had calculated; and at length Faust brought a suit to recover what he had lent. The judge decided in his favour, and everything that the inventor owned went to him. Gutenberg was left to begin again. Nevertheless he went on bravely with his printing, trying all the time to print better and better. By and by the

Elector[1] Adolphus of Nassau gave him a pension. This is all that is known of the last few years of his life. He died in 1468; but the art of printing lived. Printing presses could hardly be set up fast enough, for every country wanted them. England, France, Holland, Germany had presses within a few years after the death of Gutenberg. The Jews carried one to Constantinople, and a century later even Russia had one.

GUTENBERG SHOWING HIS FIRST PROOF

So it was that the knowledge of printing spread over Europe. Of course those old Greek manuscripts were printed and sent from country to

[1] The Electors were German princes who were allowed to choose the Emperor.

country. A Venetian printer named Aldo Manuzio issued especially accurate and well-made copies, which became known as the Aldine editions. The crusades had aroused people and made them ready and eager to learn. Now they found in the ancient writings of the Greeks and Romans nobler poems, more dignified histories, and more brilliant orations than they had known before. By this "New Learning," as it was called, men were stimulated to think. They felt as if they were brighter and keener than they used to be, as if they were not their old slow, dull selves, but were becoming quick and clear-minded. They felt so much as if they had just been born into a new, fresh world that the name Renaissance or new birth, has been given to this period.

OLDEST KNOWN PICTURE
OF A PRINTING PRESS

CHAPTER XXXIV

CHRISTOPHER COLUMBUS

THE crusades, the Renaissance, the invention of printing, and the travels of Marco Polo in the East had set people to thinking about matters in the great world beyond the limits of their own little villages or towns. India was especially attractive to many. The reason was that Europeans had learned to demand the spices and silks and cottons and jewels of the East. The old way of bringing these to Europe was up the Red Sea and across the Mediterranean to Venice; or through the Black Sea, past Constantinople, and through the Mediterranean to Genoa. Now that the Turks held Constantinople, communication with the East was made very difficult. Just as people were beginning to desire Eastern luxuries, it became more and more difficult to obtain them; and the nation that could find the shortest way to India would soon be possessed of untold wealth.

One man who was thinking most earnestly about India was named Christopher Columbus. He was born in Genoa and had been at sea most of his life since he was fourteen. He had read and studied

COLUMBUS BEFORE THE LEARNED MEN OF SALAMANCA

and thought until he was convinced that the world was round and that the best way to reach China and Japan was not to make the wearisome overland journey through Asia, but to sail directly west across the Atlantic. He had asked the city of Genoa to provide money for the expedition; and he had also asked the king of Portugal; but to no purpose. Finally he appealed to Ferdinand and Isabella, king and queen of Spain.

This was why, toward the end of the fifteenth century, a company of learned Spaniards met together at Salamanca to listen to the schemes of a simple, unknown Italian sailor. Columbus told them what he believed. Then they brought forward their objections. "A ship might possibly reach India in that way," said one gravely, "but she could never sail uphill and come home again." "If the world is round and people are on the opposite side, they must hang by their feet with their heads down," declared another scornfully. Another objection was that such an expedition as Columbus proposed would be expensive. Moreover he demanded the title of admiral of whatever lands he might discover and one tenth of all precious stones, gold, silver, spices, and other merchandise that should be found in these lands. This was not because he was greedy for money, but he had conceived the notion of winning the Holy Sepulchre at Jerusalem from the Turks, and to do this would require an enormous fortune.

Columbus had formed a noble scheme, but there seemed small hope that it would be carried out by Spanish aid, for the Spaniards were waging an important war with the Moors, or Mohammedans. The Moors had a kingdom in the south of Spain containing a number of cities. In the capital, Granada, was the palace and fortress of the Alhambra, a wonderfully beautiful structure, even in ruins as it is to-day. Granada was captured, but even then the Spaniards seemed to have no time to listen to Columbus.

CONVENT OF LA RABIDA
(The part Columbus knew is to the right)

At length he made up his mind to leave Spain and go for aid to the king of France. With his little son Diego he started out on foot. The child was hungry, and so they stopped at the gate of the convent of La Rabida, near the town of Palos, Spain, to beg for the food that was never refused to wayfarers. The prior was a student of geography. He heard the ideas of Columbus, put faith in them, and invited some of his learned friends to meet the stranger. "Spain must not lose the honour of such an enterprise," the prior declared, and he even went himself to the queen. He had once been her confessor, and she greeted him kindly. King Ferdinand did not believe in the undertaking, but the queen became thoroughly interested in it. She was Queen of Ara-

SHIPS OF COLUMBUS
(The vessels were the Pinta, the Niña, and the Santa Maria)

gon by her marriage to Ferdinand, but she was Queen of Castile in her own right, and she exclaimed, "I undertake the enterprise for my own crown of Castile, and will pledge my jewels to raise the necessary funds."

Thus, after eighteen years' delay, the way opened for Columbus, and he set sail from Palos with three small vessels; but even after they were at sea Columbus must have felt as if his troubles were but just begun, for his sailors were full of fears. They were not cowards, but no one, they thought, had ever crossed the Atlantic, and there were legends that in one place it was swarming with monsters, and that in another the water boiled with intense heat. There was real danger, also, from the jealous Portuguese, for it was rumored that they had sent out vessels to capture Columbus's little fleet. It is small wonder that the sailors were dismayed by the fires of the volcanic peak of Teneriffe, but they were almost equally alarmed by every little occurrence. The mast of a wrecked vessel floated by, and they feared it was a sign that their vessel, too, would be wrecked. After a while, the magnetic needle ceased to point to the north star, and they were filled with dread lest they should lose their way on the vast ocean. One night a brilliant meteor appeared, and then they were sure that destruction was at hand. The good east wind was sweeping them gently along; but even that worried them, for they feared it would never alter, and how could they get home? Some of them had begun to whisper together of throwing Columbus overboard, when one day they saw land-birds and floating weeds and finally a glimmering light. Then the sailors were as eager to press onward as their leader.

COLUMBUS'S FIRST VIEW OF THE NEW WORLD

Early on the following morning land appeared. Columbus wearing his brilliant scarlet robes and bearing the standard of Spain, was rowed ashore. He fell upon his knees and kissed the ground, thanking God most heartily for his care. Then he took possession of the land for Spain. The natives gathered around, and he gave them bells and glass beads. He supposed that of course he was just off the coast of India, and as he had reached the place by sailing west, he called it the West Indies and the people Indians. The island itself he named San

Salvador. It is thought to have been one of the Bahamas. He spent some little time among the islands, always hoping to come upon the wealthy cities of the Great Khan. At length he returned to Spain, dreaming of future voyages that he would make.

COLUMBUS NARRATES THE STORY OF HIS DISCOVERIES
R. Balaca

When he reached Palos, the bells were rung and people gave up their business to celebrate the wonderful voyage and the safe return. Columbus made three other journeys across the ocean, hoping every time to find the rich cities of the East. His enemies claimed that he had mismanaged a colony that had been founded in the New World. Another governor was sent out, and he threw the great Admiral into chains. Ferdinand and Isabella were indignant when they knew of this outrage; but yet they could not help being disappointed that China had not been found. Neither they nor Columbus dreamed that he had discovered a new continent; and even if they had known it, they would have much preferred finding a way to trade with the distant East.

CHAPTER XXXV

VASCO DA GAMA

W E have seen that Portugal missed the honour of sending out Columbus, although the people of that age scarcely realized that it was an honour. Six years after he crossed the Atlantic Ocean, a Portuguese sailor named Vasco da Gama made a voyage that was looked upon as being of far more importance, because it opened the way for trade with the far East for which merchants had been longing. He reached India by sailing around Africa. Navigators were already familiar with the western coast of Africa, and a few years earlier one of them had doubled the Cape of Good Hope; but of what lay beyond little was known.

Vasco da Gama, therefore, had been chosen by the king of Portugal to sail down the western coast, round the Cape of Good Hope, and then sail north up the eastern coast. When the day of departure had come, Da Gama and the men of the fleet and the courtiers all went down to the water's edge. The ships were ablaze with flags and standards. A farewell salute was fired, and the vessels floated down the river of Lisbon and out into the open sea.

On the voyage there were tempests and stormy winds, and the sea was rough day and night. When at last they thought that they must have sailed as far south as the southern point of Africa, they steered directly east. Alas, the shore soon came in sight. "There is no end to the land," declared the sailors, "it goes straight across the ocean." "Stand out to sea," commanded Da Gama. "Trust in the Lord, and we will double the Cape." On they went. The days grew shorter, the nights grew longer, and the cold rains fell constantly. Now the ships began to leak, and the men could never cease pumping. There was so little hope of safety that they no longer called upon God to save their lives, but begged Him to have mercy upon their souls. In the midst of all the distress, Da Gama strode about the ship, angry and fearless. "If we do not double the Cape this time," he declared, "we will stand out to sea again; and we will stand out as many times until the Cape is doubled, or until whatever may please God has come to pass."

By and by the sea grew calm, the wind moderated, and, however far they went to the east, no land was in sight. Then they knew that they had doubled the Cape. They were full of joy, and they praised the Lord, who had delivered them from death.

The Christmas season was at hand, which the Portuguese call Natal. They gave this name to the part of the coast off which they lay, and it has been so called ever since that time. After the shattered vessels had been repaired, Da Gama sailed onward up the coast of Africa as far as Melinda. There he found a native pilot who guided his ships across the Indian Ocean to Calicut, in Hindustan. After many adventures he returned to Portugal. The king gave him generous rewards, made him a noble, and bade that holidays should be celebrated in his honour throughout the kingdom.

Da Gama made two other voyages to India. On one of these he led a fleet of twelve ships and brought them back richly laden with spices and silks and ivory and precious stones. Finally he was made viceroy of India; and there he lived in much luxury and magnificence until his death.

For a time, the voyages of Columbus were almost forgotten. Vasco da Gama had found the way to India, and several countries of Europe, especially Portugal, were becoming rich by their trade with the East. What more could be asked?

CHAPTER XXXVI

FERDINAND MAGELLAN

W HEN the year 1519 had come, people knew much more about the world than had been known thirty years earlier. Other voyagers had followed Columbus. Vasco da Gama had sailed around Africa and shown that it was quite possible to reach India by that method. Several other bold mariners had crossed the Atlantic and explored different parts of the American coast. One had crossed the Isthmus of Darien and had seen the Pacific Ocean. It was known, therefore, that there was land from Labrador to Brazil, but no one guessed how far to the west it extended. Most people thought that the islands visited by Columbus and probably the lands north of them lay off the coast of China. No one had been around South America, but even those who thought it to be a great mass of land supposed that somewhere there was a strait leading through it to the Chinese waters. No one guessed that the wide Pacific Ocean lay between this land and China, for no one had yet carried out Columbus's plan of reaching India by sailing west.

This, however, was just what a bold navigator named Ferdinand Magellan was hoping to do. He was a Portuguese, but his own king would not send out the expedition he was planning; therefore he entered the service of the king of Spain. This daring sailor did not know any better than others how far South America might extend to the southward, but he promised the king that he would follow the coast

until he came to some strait that led through the land to the Chinese seas. He was not going merely to make discoveries; he meant to bring home whole shiploads of spices. He knew how cheaply they could be bought of the natives, and he expected to make fortunes for the king

MAGELLAN

and for himself. No one knew how long the voyage would take, but the ships were provisioned for two years. They carried also all kinds of weapons and vast quantities of bells and knives and red cloth and small looking-glasses, which they intended to exchange for spices with the natives.

The vessels crossed the Atlantic and sailed into the mouth of the Rio de la Plata. Then everyone was hopeful. "This must be a strait," they thought, "and we are almost at our journey's end." They sailed cheerfully up stream for two days. Then their hopes fell, for the water grew more fresh every hour, and therefore they knew that they were in a river; so they turned back and continued their voyage along the coast. By and by they came to another opening; this might be the passage, and Magellan sent two of the ships to explore it. When they returned, there was rejoicing indeed, for the captains reported that at last a deep channel had been found. This was surely the passage to the seas of China. But the ships were shattered and food was scanty. Since the passage had been found, why not return to Spain? The following season they could set out with new, strong vessels and a good supply of food. So said some of the captains and pilots; but others felt that the hardest part of the voyage was over, China must be close at hand, and they might just as well go home with shiploads of cloves and other spices.

On Magellan went, through the straits later named after him, into the calm, blue ocean, so quiet that he called it the Pacific. He sailed on and on. When he entered this ocean, he had food for only three months, and two months had passed. Now the explorers had no choice about turning back, for they had not provisions for a homeward voyage, and their only hope was that by keeping on they might come to the shores of India. At length they did reach a little island, but it had neither water nor fruit. They came to a group of islands, and these they named the Ladrones, or thieves' islands, because the natives stole everything they could lay their hands upon. Then they landed at the Philippines, and here was plenty of fruit,—oranges, bananas, and cocoanuts. They were now in the land of cloves, but unfortunately Magellan agreed to help one native chief against his enemies, and in the fighting that followed, he was slain.

The little fleet had at first consisted of five vessels; but one had deserted, one had been wrecked, one had been burned as unseaworthy, and one had fallen into the hands of the Portuguese. The *Victoria*, the only one that remained, pressed on to the Moluccas; and when she sailed away, she had such a cargo as no vessel had brought before, for besides all that the men had bought for themselves, she carried twenty-six tons of cloves. From some of the other islands they took ginger and sandal wood. Then they crossed the Indian Ocean and rounded Africa. They stopped to buy food at the Cape Verde Islands, and here they were astounded to find that while they called the day Wednesday, the people on the Islands called it Thursday. They had travelled west with the sun, and so had lost a day. At length they reached Spain, and there they received a royal reception. After Magellan's death, Sebastian del Cano had become captain. The courage and perseverance that had made the voyage possible belonged to Magellan; but he was dead, and the rewards went to Del Cano. He was made a noble, and for a coat of arms he was given a globe with the motto, "You first encompassed me."

During the two hundred years when Europe was making especially rapid progress in learning and in discovery, some of the noblest painters that the world has ever known, lived in Italy. One of these died while Magellan was slowly making his way around the southern point of South America. This was Raphael. His most famous picture is the Sistine Madonna, now in the Dresden Gallery, the Mother of Christ with the Holy Child in her arms. Raphael is said to have thanked God that he was born in the times of Michel Angelo, a brother artist. Angelo was painter and poet, but greatest of all as sculptor. His most famous statue is that of Moses. This is so wonderfully life-like that one feels as if it must be alive. It is easy to believe that, when it was completed, the artist gazed upon it and cried, "Speak, for thou canst." Angelo lived to be an old man, but till almost the last day of his life he was occupied with some work of art of such rare excellence that every one who loves beautiful things is glad of its existence.

CHAPTER XXXVII

ROBERT BRUCE

IN the days of King John, the English had their hands full with only one king to manage, but a time came in Scotland when there were thirteen persons who claimed the throne. Finally it was clear that two of them had stronger claims than the other eleven. They were John Baliol and Robert Bruce. Baliol was the grandson of the eldest daughter of a certain royal David, and Bruce was a son of the second daughter of this same king. People in Scotland took sides, some in favour of Baliol and some in favour of Bruce, and feeling was so strong that there was danger of civil war. "King Edward of England is a wise king. Let us leave the question to him," said the Scottish nobles, and it was done. This was a fine chance for King Edward. He declared at once that neither Baliol nor Bruce, but he himself had the best claim to the Scottish throne. Baliol, however, might rule under him, he said. But Baliol did not prove obedient enough to please him, so Edward carried him and the famous Stone of Scone off to London together. The Scots prized the Stone highly. They had a tradition that Jacob's head had rested upon it the night that he had his dream of angels ascending and descending between heaven and earth; and whenever a Scottish king was to be crowned, he always took his seat upon this stone. Edward had it put underneath the seat of the chair in Westminster Abbey, in which English sovereigns sit at their coronation; and perhaps he thought that Scotland had yielded, and there would be no more trouble. On the contrary, in a very little while William Wallace led the Scots against the English and defeated them in a great battle. Soon after this, however, he fell into the hands of Edward and was put to death.

EDWARD I.

After a few years the Scots found a new leader. This was the grandson of Robert Bruce, and his name, too, was Robert Bruce. He was crowned King of Scotland, and the Scots flocked to his standard. Then came Edward with a large force, and soon the King of Scotland was hiding first in the Grampian Hills, then on a little island off the north coast of Ireland. He was almost in despair, for he had tried six times to get the better of the English and had failed. One day, it is said, he lay in a lonely hut on a heap of straw, wondering if it would not be better to give it up and leave Scotland to herself. Just then he caught sight of a spider trying to swing itself from one rafter to another. Six times it tried, and six times it failed. "Just as many times as I have failed," thought Bruce, and he said to himself, "If it tries again and succeeds, I, too, will try again." The spider tried again and it succeeded. Bruce tried again, and he, too, succeeded. Edward died, and before his son Edward II. was ready to attend to matters in Scotland, Bruce had captured most of the castles that Edward I. had taken and had brought an army together.

CORONATION CHAIR WITH STONE OF SCONE

When Edward II. was at last ready to march into Scotland, some two or three years later, he came with a large force as far as Stirling. Bruce met him with one only one-third as large, but every man in it was bent upon doing his best to drive away the English. Bruce dug deep pits in front of his lines. Many of the English cavalry plunged into these and were slain, and the rest were thrown into confusion. Then as the English troops looked at the hill lying to the right of the Scottish army, they saw a new army coming over the crest. It was really only the servants and wagons and camp followers; but Bruce had given them plenty of banners, and the English supposed they were fresh troops. Then King Edward and his men ran away as fast as they could; but the Scots pursued, and the king barely escaped being taken prisoner. This was the Battle of Bannockburn, the most bloody defeat that the English ever met with in Scotland. The victory of the Scots freed Scotland

BATTLE OF BANNOCKBURN

from all English claims; and a few years later England acknowledged her independence.

It was of this battle that Robert Burns, wrote:—

Scots, wha hae wi' Wallace bled,
Scots, wham Bruce has aften led;
Welcome to your gory bed,
　　Or to victory!
Now's the day, and now's the hour;
See the front o' battle lour;
See approach proud Edward's power—
　　Chains and slavery!

Wha will be a traitor knave?
Wha can fill a coward's grave?
Wha sae base as be a slave?
　　Let him turn and flee!
Wha for Scotland's king and law
Freedom's sword will strongly draw,
Freeman stand, or Freeman fa',
　　Let him follow me!

By oppression's woes and pains!
By your sons in servile chains!
We will drain our dearest veins,
　　But they shall be free!
Lay the proud usurpers low!
Tyrants fall in every foe!
Liberty's in every blow!—
　　Let us do, or die!

In 1603 James VI. of Scotland became James I. of England, but although for the next hundred years the kingdoms were ruled by the same sovereign, the parliaments were not united. This followed, however, in 1707, England and Scotland were henceforth one country under the name of Great Britain.

CHAPTER XXXVIII

THE STORIES OF WILLIAM TELL AND ARNOLD VON WINKELRIED

I N early times, some tall, strong people who had light hair, blue eyes, and fair complexions took up their homes in Switzerland. They were a proud, independent race; and proudest of all were those who dwelt in three districts far up in the mountains, known later as the Forest Cantons. Even after those who lived in the lower parts of the land had been obliged to give up much of their liberty, the Forest Cantons were still free. They yielded to the Emperor of Germany, they said, and to no one else.

At one time Rudolph of the family of Hapsburg was emperor. He was of Swiss birth. He loved his people and protected them; but after him came his son Albert, a cruel tyrant. He was determined to bring the Swiss under the rule of Austria, and he was especially bitter against the Forest Cantons. He set governors over them who were free to insult the people, steal from them, imprison them, or even put them to death. The worst of all the governors was a man named Gessler, and the land was full of tales of his insolence and wickedness.

Gessler seemed determined to humble the Swiss in every possible way. One day he put an Austrian hat on a pole and set it up in the market-place with the command that every one who passed should bow down to it as if it were the emperor himself. William Tell, a bold mountaineer, walked through the place with his little son, and did not salute the hat, wherefore he was seized by the guards. Gessler, in cruel sport, told him that since he carried a bow, he might display his archery by shooting an apple from the head of his son, and if he succeeded in doing it without killing the child his own life should be spared. Tell pleaded not to be compelled to make so unnatural a trial, but the tyrant forced him to do it. The mountaineer was a skilful archer, and he hit the apple, to the great joy of all the people who stood round; but Gessler had noticed that Tell had taken another arrow in his hand, and he demanded suspiciously, "Why did you take out a second arrow?" Tell replied boldly, "If I had slain my child this should have found your heart." Gessler was furious. He threw Tell into chains and that night started to take him across the Lake of the Four Cantons to a prison on the other side. It is not at all uncommon for a storm to rise suddenly amidst the mountains that surround the beautiful lake. Without warning the waters will be lashed into fury, and woe betide the boats that are not lying safely at anchor. Such a storm now overtook Gessler and his com-

THE STATUE OF TELL AT ALTDORF

pany. "Tell knows the lake, and he is the only man that can save us," declared the peasants who were rowing. "Unbind him, then!" bade the frightened governor, "and give him the helm." Tell did know the lake and he guided the boat through the darkness to where a rock jutted out into the water. Coming as near as he dared, he made a bold spring to the rock, gave a thrust to the boat, and in a moment was free on the land while Gessler and his men were fighting for their lives to prevent the boat from being swamped. Eventually the governor was saved, but the next day he and his escort had to pass through some deep woods. He was exclaiming, "Let him surrender, or one of his children dies to-morrow, another on the second day, and his wife on the third," when suddenly an arrow whizzed through the branches, and the tyrant fell dead. Whether the arrow came from Tell's bow, no one knew.

Before this some of the bold mountaineers had met under the stars one night on a little point that stretched out into a lake, and had sworn to stand together to free themselves from the tyranny of the Hapsburgs. The duke himself came with an army to subdue the rebellious Swiss; but as his troops were marching through a deep, narrow pass, suddenly rocks and trunks of trees were hurled down upon them. Then came the Swiss with their clubs and pikes, and the proud Austrians were overpowered and driven back by the mountain peasants.

Again, some seventy years later, the Austrians tried to conquer Switzerland. When the moment of battle had come, the knights dismounted and stood with their long spears in rest, a wall of bristling steel. The Swiss had only swords and short spears, and they could not even reach their enemies. The Austrians were beginning to curve their lines so as to surround the Swiss, when Arnold von Winkelried, a brave Swiss, suddenly cried, "My comrades, I will open a way for you!" and threw himself upon the lances, clasping in his arms as many as he could and dragging them to the ground. In an instant his comrades sprang into the opening. The Austrians fought gallantly, but they were routed. It was by such struggles as these that Switzerland freed herself from the yoke of Austria.

These two stories have been handed down in Switzerland from father to son for many years. People doubt their truth; but in one way at least there is truth in them; namely, they show how earnestly the Swiss loved liberty. They came to hate everything connected with Austria, even peacock feathers, because they were the symbol of Austria. It is said that once an ardent patriot was drinking from a glass when the sun shone through it and the detested colours appeared. Straightway the man dashed the glass to the floor, and it was shattered into a thousand pieces.

DEATH OF ARNOLD VON WINKELRIED

CHAPTER XXXIX

EDWARD THE BLACK PRINCE

THE war between England and Scotland, which ended with the Battle of Bannock-burn, would not have lasted so long if the French had not feared the growing strength of England. They had done a great deal to help Scotland, and this did not make the English feel very friendly toward them. Moreover, Edward III., King of England, claimed the French crown, because of his relationship to the late king of France. The result was a struggle which lasted more than a century, and which is, therefore, called the Hundred Years' War. It was in the early part of this war that the famous battles of Crécy and Poitiers were fought, which showed the English yeomen—that is, the sturdy common people—that they could defend themselves with their bows and arrows, and could stand up in battle without protection from the knights. At the battle of Crécy, King Edward shared the command with his son, called the Black Prince from the colour of his armour. In the course of the battle, a messenger came galloping up to the king and told him that his son was in great danger. "If the Frenchmen increase, your son will have too much to do," he said. The king asked, "Is my son dead, unhorsed, or so badly wounded that he cannot support himself?" "No, sire," answered the messenger, "but he is in so hot an engagement that he has great need of your help." The king must have longed to go to his son, but he replied firmly, "Tell those that sent you not to send again for me so long as my son has life; and say I command them to let the boy win his spurs; for I am determined, if it please God, that all the glory and honour of this day shall be given to him and to those to whose care I have entrusted him." The brave prince did win his spurs, that is, he performed deeds which proved him worthy of knighthood; and when the battle was over the king kissed him and said, "You are worthy to be a sovereign."

After this battle, the English pressed on to besiege Calais. One whole year the French refused to yield, and they would not give up the town until they were starving. Edward was so angry at the long resistance that he told the people of Calais there was only one way in which they could look for any mercy from him. If six of their principal men would come to him in their shirts, bareheaded, barefooted, and with ropes about their necks, he would be merciful to the others. The

EDWARD III.
(From a wall painting, formerly in Westminster Abbey)

richest man in town offered himself first, and five others followed. "Take them away and hang them," commanded King Edward; but his wife Philippa fell upon her knees and said, "Since I crossed the sea with great danger to see you, I have never asked you one favour. Now I most humbly ask for the sake of

QUEEN PHILIPPA PLEADING FOR THE MEN OF CALAIS

the Son of the Blessed Mary, and for your love to me that you will be merciful to these six men." The king replied, "Ah, lady, I wish you had been any-where else than here, but I cannot refuse you. Do as you please with them." The queen feasted them, and gave them new clothes and sent them back safely to their homes. This story was told by Queen Philippa's secretary, a man named Froissart, who wrote a famous history of the time, which is known as *Frois-sart's Chronicles*.

Froissart tells another story about the courtesy

and modesty of the Black Prince after the French king had been taken prisoner at the battle of Poitiers. Here it is just as the old chronicler told it:—

"The Prince of Wales gave a supper in his pavilion to the king of France and to the greater part of the princes and barons who were prisoners. The prince seated the king of France and his son, the Lord Philip, at an elevated and well-covered table. With them were Sir James de Bourbon, the Lord John d'Artois, the earls of Tancarville, of Estampes, of Dammartin, of Granville, and the lord of Partenay. The other knights and squires were placed at different tables. The prince himself served the king's table as well as the others with every mark of humility, and would not sit down at it, in spite of all his entreaties for him so to do, saying that he was not worthy of such an honour, nor did it appertain to him to seat himself at the table of so great a king, or of so valiant a man as he had shown himself by his actions that day. He added, also, with a noble air, 'Dear sir, do not make a poor meal because the Almighty God has not gratified your wishes in the event of this day; for be assured that my lord and father will show

TOMB OF THE BLACK PRINCE, IN CANTERBURY CATHEDRAL

(His helmet, shield, and shirt of mail are shown above)

you every honour and friendship in his power, and will arrange your ransom so reasonably that you will henceforward always remain friends. In my opinion, you have cause to be glad that the success of this battle did not turn out as you desired; for you have this day acquired such high renown for prowess that you have surpassed all the best knights on your side. I do not, dear sir, say this to flatter you, for all those of our side who have seen and observed the actions of each party have unanimously allowed this to be your due, and decree you the prize and garland for it.' At the end of this speech there were murmurs of praise heard from every one. And the French said the prince had spoken nobly and truly; and that he would be one of the most gallant princes in Christendom if God should grant him life to pursue his career of glory."

The Black Prince never came to the throne, for he died one year before his father. If he had lived, his courage and gentleness and kindly tact might have prevented some of the troubles that England had to meet.

CHAPTER XL

JOAN OF ARC

THE Hundred Years' War was renewed when Henry V. came to the throne, and by his great victory at Agincourt in 1415 France was quite at his mercy. At length the French became so discouraged that they agreed that when their king should die they would accept an English ruler. The daughter of the French king was married to Henry, who died shortly afterwards. At the death of Henry V. the new king of England was a little boy. His guardians tried to enforce his claims, and they invaded France. They succeeded in getting possession of Northern France, but they could not press farther into the country without capturing Orleans. This they made strong efforts to do; they laid siege to the city; it grew weaker and weaker, and all saw that it must soon fall into their hands.

The French were good soldiers, but they needed a leader. They were fighting for the rights of the young king Charles, but it did not seem to enter his mind that he should do aught except wear the crown after they had captured it for him. At length word came that a young peasant girl named Joan, from Domrémy insisted upon seeing him. She declared that she had seen visions of angels and had heard voices bidding her raise the siege of Orleans and conduct the king to Rheims to be crowned.

She was brought before the king; but he had dressed himself more plainly than his courtiers to see if she would recognize him. She looked about her a moment, then knelt before him. "I am not the king," said Charles. "Noble prince, you and no one else, are the king," Joan responded; and she told him of the voices that she had heard. Now, there was an old saying in France that some day the country would be saved by a maiden, and both king and courtiers became interested. They gave her some light armour, all white and shining, and set her upon a great white charger with a sword in her hand. Her banner was a standard of pure white, and on it was a picture of two angels bearing lilies and one of God holding up the world. The French were wild with enthusiasm. They fell down before her, and those who could come near enough to touch her armour or even her horse's hoofs thought themselves fortunate. Joan of Arc, as she is known in history, was only seventeen, and she had seen nothing of war, but she succeeded in leading the French troops into Orleans. When once she had made her way within the walls, the French shut up in the city began to believe that she was sent by Heaven to save them. She bade them follow her to do battle with the English, and they obeyed joyfully. The English had heard of this. Some thought she was, indeed, sent by Heaven; others said she was a witch; and they were all half afraid

JOAN OF ARC
Stephen Reid

to resist her. It was not long before they withdrew. The city was free; and the French were almost ready to worship the "Maid of Orleans," as they called her. They were eager to follow wherever she led; and with every battle the English were driven a little farther to the northward.

Joan now urged Charles to go to Rheims to be crowned; but he held back. So did his brave old generals. "It is folly," they said, "to try to make our way through a country where the English are still in power. Let us first drive them from Normandy and from Paris. Let the coronation wait until we have possession of our capital." Still Joan begged Charles to go, and at length he yielded. There was much fighting on the way, but the French were victorious, and Joan led her king to Rheims. He was crowned in the cathedral, and she stood near him, the white war banner in her hand.

Then Joan prayed to be allowed to go home; but Charles would not think of giving her up. His people had come to believe that they would win a victory wherever she led; they even fancied that they saw fire flashing around her standard. "I work no miracles," she declared. "Do not kiss my clothes or armour. I am nothing but the instrument that God uses." She continued to lead the army, but at length she was captured and fell into the hands of the English. Those were hard and cruel days, and the English fired cannon and sang the *Te Deum* in the churches and rejoiced as if they had conquered the whole kingdom of France.

Joan was kept in prison for a year, loaded with irons and chained to a pillar. She was tried for witch-craft and was condemned and sentenced to be burned. Charles, to whom she had given a kingdom, made no effort to save her. A stake was set up in the market-place of Rouen. To this she was bound, and fagots were heaped up around it. "Let me die with the cross in my hands," she pleaded; but no one paid any attention to her request, until at length an English soldier tied two sticks together in the form of a cross and gave it to her. She kissed it and laid it upon her heart. Then a brave and kindly monk ventured to bring her the altar cross from a church near at hand. The flames rose around her. Those who stood near heard her say, "Jesus! Jesus!" and soon her sufferings were ended. Her ashes were thrown into the Seine, but to-day on the spot where she died a noble statue stands in her honour.

CPSIA information can be obtained
at www.ICGtesting.com
Printed in the USA
BVHW03s1718140718
521642BV00001B/64/P

9 781599 151694